Higher Education in 2040

Higher Education in 2040

A Global Approach

Bert van der Zwaan

AUP

The publication of this book is made possible by a grant from Utrecht University.

Also published in Dutch: Bert van der Zwaan, *Haalt de universiteit 2040? Een Europees perspecties op wereldwijde kansen en bedreigingen* (ISBN 978 94 6298 415 8)

Translation: Vivien Collingwood

Photo back cover: Arnaud Mooij
Cover design: Wat ontwerpers
Lay-out: Crius Group, Hulshout

Amsterdam University Press English-language titles are distributed in the US and Canada by the University of Chicago Press.

ISBN	978 94 6298 450 9
e-ISBN	978 90 4853 516 3 (pdf)
e-ISBN	978 90 4853 517 0 (ePub)
NUR	740

Preface

The university is one of the oldest institutions in the world. After eight hundred years, it is still going strong where many other institutions have foundered. The university even appears to be flourishing: in the Netherlands for instance, as elsewhere, student numbers continue to rise, the research enjoys a good reputation and Dutch universities' results are impressive – certainly if one takes the size of the country into consideration.

Nevertheless, these are turbulent times. There is criticism from all sides: criticism of the mass nature of education, the focus on efficiency and research output, the lack of collaboration with industry, and the relatively meagre attention that universities are said to pay to societal problems. And that is just criticism from the outside world. Within the university community, the voices of lecturers and students can also be heard. They are often critical of administrators, 'who have transformed the university into a factory'.

As well as criticisms of the current situation, there are also challenges for the future. Information technology is leading to rapid changes in teaching and research. Across the world, it seems that university teaching is gradually being privatized and governments are no longer automatically funding research. The labour market is set to change fundamentally, and with this, education for students. What is more, the world faces major problems when it comes to distributing dwindling supplies of food, energy, water and raw materials across a growing global population. This, too, means that the university faces new questions and, no doubt, new responsibilities.

How is the university tackling the existing problems and how is it preparing for the future? Where will the pressures and opportunities lie in the coming 25 years? Or, to put it differently: how can the university best survive? In this collection of essays, I search for answers to these questions. Owing to its form, the book became a kaleidoscopic exploration rather than a systematic study. Many of the essays are based on blogs, columns and speeches that were originally written from a global perspective. The emphasis has shifted slightly in this collection, in that I make comparisons between Europe on the one hand and North America and Asia on the other. I do not consider other parts of the world, because comparing these three continents already proved complex enough. In practice, the emphasis of the essays is not on the whole of Europe, which proved impossible, but on Western Europe and England, whilst for Asia, I focus on China, Hong Kong and Singapore. When it comes to North America, I discuss a relatively large number of problems affecting the US. Here and there, I sharpen the focus a little by referring to the current debate in the Netherlands. In some respects, this differs from the discourse unfolding at the European level. It is striking here that student activism is throwing the issues the university is struggling with into much starker relief than elsewhere. I attempt to explain this difference, among other things, with reference to the specific agreements that the universities made with the Dutch government.

Although I have attempted to present a balanced discussion of all aspects of the university system, there is somewhat more of an emphasis on research universities. The various international comprehensive universities are easy to compare, whereas the other parts of the system of higher education differ greatly from one country to the next. In the Netherlands, for example, there is a clear separation between the research-intensive university on the one hand and the 'applied university' or 'polytechnic' on the other, while in other countries these are all part of the same system. As a result, while they are all referred to as universities, there are significant differences in quality, which makes it virtually impossible to effectively compare them with one another.

This book is divided into three parts. The first is the most descriptive, the two successive ones are of a more opinion-based character. In the first part, I attempt to trace the origins of the problems with which the university is grappling. On the different continents these are admittedly different problems, but we nevertheless find surprising similarities, too. It is useful to return, time and again, to the origins of today's problems, because analysing them often reveals solutions. The short, essay-like character of the analysis in this book brings a risk, however: it makes it easy for critics to point to lacunae or other explanations than offered here. This is a risk I am willing to take, particularly because the first part is also meant to offer an overview for the reader who lacks a ready knowledge of the developments within the university in recent decades; an overview that may prove helpful when reading later chapters. The different sections can also stand alone, however, and the essays can be read in a random order. To allow for this, the reader must forgive some repetition here and there.

The first part provides a conceptual framework – a springboard, as it were – for the two successive parts. In these, I state my opinions freely in an attempt to discover where the university is headed in future, whilst remaining aware that for each of the continents or even the individual countries discussed, one could add a lot of additional information that would transform the black-and-white sketch offered here to a watercolour. More than nuance, however, there is a need for a broad debate: a debate in which society and the university look one another squarely in the eye to discuss the question of what would be desirable in future, not only for the university, but also for society. We are seeing far too little of this, partly because there is such mutual distrust between the universities and the policy world and politics. I therefore wanted this book to contribute to broadening and advancing the debate. That is why I opted for short and relatively accessible essays, rather than an in-depth study, which would have run the risk of being accessible only to experts.

The chosen structure of short essays allows for accessibility and freedom of thinking. As remarked earlier, I allowed some repetition here and there so that it would be easier to read the chapters on an individual basis. However, the loose structure also requires a bit more brainwork from the reader, because rather than having a single, tight line of argument, varying perspectives are presented. This is the case, for instance, for the conceptual framework that was used. In the first part in particular, there is a strong emphasis on explaining the university and its modern problems with reference to the historical context. Already in that part, however, as well as in the second and third parts, many of the developments could be explained from an economic perspective. The debate between what is known as 'historical institutionalism' on the one hand, and 'resource dependency theory' on the other, which stresses the economic framework as the motor driving the developments within the university, has the potential to create confusion. But exploring this in more depth would have been to the detriment of the relatively short and opinion-based character of the essays.

Something similar applies to the extensive literature that exists on the differences and similarities between the continental European and Anglo-Saxon universities. In order to describe all of these nuances in detail, it would have been necessary to employ an extensive system of footnotes and concepts. In this book, these have been provided only in part. I have referred to sources for further information when necessary, but this, too, is limited to an emphasis on the main outlines. This is also the case more generally: almost everywhere, I have opted for a very limited selection of sources, mainly to keep the book readable, whilst nevertheless helping the reader on their way should more information be desired.

This collection of essays is the product of the short four-month sabbatical that I enjoyed between May and August 2015. During that period, I talked with many colleagues from around the world; it is impossible to acknowledge them all separately. Many of them were fellow rectors or university administrators, but I also spoke to interested parties from government, the private sector and NGOs. I am extremely grateful for the generous way in which they were prepared to share their knowledge with me.

It was in Spain that I first summarized and organized all of the data that I had collected during my sabbatical. In Miranda de Castañar, Govert Dibbets and Yvonne Arends offered their hospitality and allowed me to work completely undisturbed. Richard de Waard, Reinout van Brakel and Marijk van der Wende helped me to find the statistical data I needed. Annemieke Hekking provided secretarial support with finding data and checking references. Kurt Deketelaere, Peter Vale and Marijk van der Wende made special contributions in the form of long discussions, but also by providing material and numerous new insights and, last but not least, helping to organize discussions. Frank Miedema, Hans de Jonge, Esther Stiekema and Sietzke Vermeulen provided extremely helpful criticism on parts of the manuscript at an early stage; Marijk van der Wende, Kurt Deketelaere and Melanie Peters commented on the first full draft. Naturally, any errors that remain are my responsibility alone.

The sabbatical proved to be a wonderful time for my partner Wilma Wessels and myself, due to all the travelling together and the time abroad. During the whole period, we were able to do much more together than we normally can, given the busy lives that we both lead. We also talked at length about the content of this book. For both these reasons, this book is for her.

Utrecht, January 2017

Table of contents

Part 3   Contours of the university of the future

Introduction: a sinking ship?

In this collection of essays, I start by exploring the factors that led to the modern university systems with which we are familiar around the world. These different systems are experiencing different problems – which means there will often be different solutions. This also means, though, that the solutions that work in one country will not necessarily work in another. All too often in the Netherlands, for example, attempts are made to solve problems by imitating American or English universities, even though the nature of the Dutch system might make this impossible. In the second part, I identify the major challenges that the universities are facing as a result of societal changes. These can also differ by continent, or even by country. In the third part, over a number of essays, I consider the question of how universities will respond to the pressure emanating from these changing social circumstances: new threats will emerge in the coming 25 years, but also great opportunities.

Will the university make it to 2040? Many solutions have already been proposed for the problems that the university currently faces.[1,2] These solutions are often relatively abstract, however, and it is unclear whether they will work in the current system. The question we should be asking is: which key do we need to press in order to achieve real solutions? A further question is also relevant here: does it

1   Barnett, R., 2011: *Being a University*, Routledge, 188 pp. Wide-ranging study on the core values and objectives of the university.
2   Elkana, Y.& H. Klöpper, 2012: *Die Universität im 21. Jahrhundert. Für eine neue Einheit von Lehre, Forschung und Gesellschaft*, Edition Körber-Stiftung. Overview of the objectives of the modern university, mainly written from a continental European perspective, including many examples from educational practice.

actually help if we press the keys – does the university itself determine what happens? – or is the university simply a product of societal processes? The first part of this collection focuses mainly on processes within the university, and is thus concerned with the keys that the university could press in order to achieve a better balance where necessary. The second part looks in more depth at the factors lying beyond the university that will have a major impact in the coming 25 years.

It is my aim, with this collection of essays, to gradually build the impression that whilst the university is by no means a sinking ship, as some have claimed, it needs to make a clear about-turn in order to survive. Almost every aspect of its existence will be transformed. Teaching will change radically, but above all, the students who follow its educational programmes will change. No longer will a degree be the ultimate objective, but made-to-measure courses that give a good grounding for a career in a fundamentally different labour market. No longer will there be research that is mostly disciplinary, but research that is carried out in the exceptionally dynamic world of big data and changing collaborations, including digital partnerships. No longer will there be a university where financing is the leading factor, but one where contributing to the world beyond forms a leitmotif for its actions. It is troubling that the debate both with and within the universities tends to be about budget cuts or the government's vision, when it should in fact be about how we should approach the major changes that are inevitably coming. As a result, the university often lacks a broadly shared set of values with which we could tackle the problems of today and tomorrow.

In contrast to all these concerns and problems is the fact that the university is actually the most hopeful community that has ever existed, filled with young people who are looking to the future, and clever souls who are opening up new scientific horizons; a community that has shown for the last eight hundred years that it has the resilience to survive.

Part 1
Ancient problems and modern dilemmas

This part contains a succinct analysis of how and why the university came to be what it is today. Which problems were inherited from the past and have to be solved for the future? Is the basic idea of the university still tenable? Whilst the university has been successful for almost eight hundred years, the number of pressure points – which are often rooted in the past – is increasing. Today, the question is whether the government is still willing or able to fund university education: private education is on the rise around the world, often paired with increasingly stringent selection. What is more, the universities can hardly keep pace with the growth in student numbers, also in view of falling state contributions. This growth is rooted in the sharp rise in participation in higher education that began in the mid-twentieth century, when, under conditions of growing prosperity, access to university was democratized to a profound degree. Ironically enough, despite the rise in student numbers, universities are increasingly being assessed on the basis of their research, which is receiving more and more funding from third parties. This is bringing the core values that were inherited from the Enlightenment, in the form of freedom of research and the independence of the university, into question. Under pressure, the university is looking for new solutions.

1.   The idea of a university

At first sight, universities are doing better than ever. Never before have there been so many good institutions of higher education, which conduct what is often fantastic research and where students receive better teaching than ever. On closer inspection, however, the bitter wind of a fundamentally changed society is whipping around the university's ancient, originally twelfth-century, form. Many believe that the old university has been transformed into a teaching factory, where students, as modern consumers, protest against the value for money they receive. The compact institutions of the past have become large businesses in which many scholars no longer feel at home. The image of focused study in silent libraries has largely been supplanted by a deluge of complaints about the pressure of work, in a setting that is more reminiscent of the care sector than a peaceful temple of learning.

The arrows of discontented lecturers and students are aimed at administrators, for steering universities in a way comparable to the captain of the *Titanic* hitting the iceberg, or at the government, which is blamed for ever-increasing levels of bureaucracy in the universities.[1] In essence, the question that is often tabled in these frequently passionate debates is: to *whom* does the university belong? Lying behind this, however, is also the question: *what* is the university, in fact? These questions of ownership and identity have deep roots in

---

1   Ginsberg, B., 2014: 'College Presidents – New Captains of the Titanic'. *Minding the Campus*, July 2014. For the Dutch debate, see: Verbrugge, A. & J. van Baardwijk, (eds), 2014: *Waartoe is de universiteit op aarde?*, Boom, 296 pp. Provides a lot of background and information on the developments within the Dutch system, including what is often critical reflection, such as on the performance agreements that the Dutch universities concluded with the government in 2012.

the past, meaning that it is essential to have an understanding of the past in order to understand the modern predicament.

Whilst the roots of the modern university undeniably stretch back to the Middle Ages, the university in its present form is largely a product of the Enlightenment. It was in that era and after that ideas about the utility and necessity of university education were formulated. Many of the conflicts that are currently coming to light can be traced back to the question of whether these ideas are still valuable or will hold out in future. Within the university, a considerable number of lecturers and students wish to return to the ideals of the past: a significant role for teaching, and the academic atmosphere that is typical of relatively small universities. But society is demanding a number of other things as well, such as contributions to social, and above all, economic needs. It is with these and other diverse views that the university is currently grappling.

Two core nineteenth-century ideas can be seen as having played a major role in the development of the modern university: one proposed by Newman and the other by Von Humboldt. Given that both are frequently cited in the debates, it is almost self-evident that we should begin our quest with them. Building on the ideals of the Enlightenment, over 150 years ago, Cardinal John Henry Newman[2] put forward a number of pioneering ideas in his celebrated book, *The idea*

2   Newman, J.J., 1852: *The Idea of a University*. It is important to emphasize that the differences between the systems in North America and Europe are also attributable, to a significant extent, to the Land Grant Act that was passed in the US, which defined the social contract of many universities in the nineteenth century. This established a university mission that was strongly oriented towards society, whereas in Europe, particularly under Napoleon's influence, the connection with the state became progressively stronger. As a result, the core mission of American universities has traditionally been focused on contributing to the common good, much more so than in Europe.

of a university, that are still cited approvingly today. It is striking, though, that these approvingly-cited passages are often lifted unilaterally from his work by people who have obviously barely read it, as the modern university has now moved very far from the ideal picture painted by Newman – and that is a good thing! For Newman promoted the notion of a university that was totally focused on teaching, and even went so far as to describe the transfer of knowledge as the ultimate goal: 'If its [the university] object were scientific and philosophical discovery, I do not see why a university should have students.' In other words: students are the justification of the university's existence and research has no part to play.

As a good Roman Catholic, Newman was part of a long-established ecclesiastical tradition, stemming from the Middle Ages, in which the university was seen primarily as a teaching institution and the guardian of knowledge; an idea that no one would endorse today. Newman's argument remains important, though, due to his conviction that the first years of university should feature a broad educational curriculum in which students develop on the basis of their talents. Newman defended this as follows: 'All branches of knowledge are connected together, because the subject-matter of knowledge is intimately united in itself, as being the acts and the work of the Creator.' Although this would hardly be conceivable today, given the religious bent of his words, Newman's ideas had a major influence on the Anglo-Saxon model of liberal education, which aimed to provide a broad educational foundation within higher education for a career in society or possible further study in a more specialized area or discipline. And it is this notion of a broad, general education that is rapidly gaining currency in the European debate, in the wake of a long period of increasingly specialized university teaching. The textbox sets out the key similarities and differences between Europe and North America in this respect.

Key similarities and differences between the university systems in Europe and North America

In North America, the higher education system is based on colleges that provide a broad preparatory academic education, partly analogous to the Bachelor's phase in Europe. Traditionally, this phase has been highly developed in Liberal Arts and Sciences colleges; the latter distinguish themselves by providing students with a wide range of subjects from both the sciences, and the social sciences and humanities. There is great variety among the colleges. This phase of education is known as the undergraduate phase.

A limited number of the students in North America go on to the Master's programme, which is mainly seen as preparation for gaining a doctorate during the PhD phase. The entire Master's and PhD phase is known as the graduate phase.

In continental Europe, the university Bachelor's degree is not usually seen as an endpoint (at least, not yet), whereas this is often the case in North America. In Europe, the great majority of students go on to a Master's programme after obtaining their Bachelor's diploma.

There is less variety in university education (public/private, forms of education such as that provided by the colleges, different types of university) in Europe than in North America. Whereas universities in Europe often combine teaching with research, in North American we find the research university, or the comprehensive research university: the broad research university. This is in contrast to the teaching university, which focuses mainly on teaching, comparable with for instance the 'university colleges' in the Netherlands.

In terms of form, higher education in England lies between the European and the American systems.

There are significant differences in relation to what is understood as a university: whereas in the US and England, there is a gradual transition between higher vocational education and the university, in the Netherlands and the rest of Northern Europe, there is a sharp division between institutions of higher professional education, or so-called universities of applied sciences or polytechnics, and the university. In Southern Europe, too, the distinction between higher vocational education and the university has traditionally been narrower, because universities in Southern Europe have traditionally had a greater focus on preparing students for the professions than those in Northern Europe.

The form of modern Asian universities is often similar to that found in the Anglo-Saxon system.

These days, Von Humboldt is also frequently cited with enthusiasm, although here, too, the suspicion would be justified that virtually no one has actually read his work. In Europe, particularly in the Netherlands, this nineteenth-century Prussian education minister is described almost affectionately as the founder of the modern university and the inventor of the concept of 'Bildung'. But the form of education that Von Humboldt introduced as a minister in the then Prussian system was not new; it built on longstanding traditions in Western Europe. His contribution, however, was to institutionalize these traditions by arguing that good university education was characterized by the constant linking of teaching and research, whereby students had to be educated and trained ('Bildung') in a system that prioritized the acquisition of new knowledge. As he wrote in 1810:

> Es ist ferner eine Eigenthümlichkeit der höheren wissenschaftlichen Anstalten, dass sie die Wissenschaft immer als ein noch nicht ganz aufgelöstes Problem behandeln und daher immer im Forschen bleiben, da die Schule es nur mit fertigen und abgemachten Kenntnissen zu thun hat und lernt. Das

Verhältniss zwischen Lehrer und Schüler wird daher durchaus ein anderes als vorher. Der erstere ist nicht für die letzteren, Beide sind für die Wissenschaft da.[3]

In other words, this was about much more than merely transferring existing knowledge – something for which Newman was still calling some forty years later.

Four problems with historical roots

The university has undergone a complete transformation since the days of Newman and Von Humboldt, and many of their ideas are simply no longer relevant. Despite this, they are frequently invoked in the current debate about 'why we have universities at all'. In Europe, in particular, a sizeable movement can be seen and heard that believes that the university is focusing too strongly on research to the detriment of teaching. In his book, *What are universities for?*, Stefan Collini,[4] for example, argues for a return to old values and a greater emphasis on teaching. Others, such as

3   Von Humboldt, W., 1810: *Über die innere und äußere Organisation der höheren wissenschaftlichen Anstalten in Berlin.* The quote could be translated as follows: 'It is furthermore a quality of higher scholarly institutions that they treat science as a problem that remains unsolved as of yet, and therefore always should remain inquisitive, because (normal) schools are only concerned with and teach cut-and-dried knowledge. The relationship between teacher and pupil is thus very different from how it was in the past: the former is not only there for the latter, but both are there for science.'
4   Collini, S., 2012: *What Are Universities For?*, Penguin Books. Critical analysis, written mainly from the perspective of the humanities in the context of an elite university.

Crow and Dabars,[5] argue to the contrary that it is vital to preserve a strong emphasis on research in the context of the modern research university. It is this question of the balance between the two that lies at the heart of the modern debate.

The second question, which gives rise to sharp differences of opinion, can also essentially be traced back to nineteenth-century views that are now coming under heavy pressure. Von Humboldt was an outspoken defender of a well-ordered polity, something for which Prussia was famous at the time. Within this tradition, in Germany and many other European countries there was for many years no debate about who should pay for the university: this was obviously the task of the state. Thus it is perhaps no coincidence that Newman, who wanted to found a Roman Catholic university – a private university, in other words – enjoyed so much influence in the US and in England: in these university systems, the state has traditionally played a much weaker role, and has even been notably absent in many respects. Take the American universities, which are privately funded to a great extent and where the government plays a modest role in funding higher education. This means that universities in the US and in England, to an extent, face very different problems from those in continental Europe. On both continents, however, and probably in Asia as well in future, how to fund the university is an extremely important and growing problem.

While the third focus of discontent within modern universities cannot be traced back directly to the Enlightenment, it is related to it; for it was from this time onwards, in principle, that the democratization of access to the university,

5   Crow, Michael M. & William B. Dabars, 2015: *Designing the New American University*, John Hopkins University Press. Analysis of the situation of the universities in the US, paying significant attention to rising costs, government withdrawal, and the implications for the social divide in the US.

or 'education for the many', in modern jargon, became anchored. Since the days of Von Humboldt and Newman, the university system has been subject to constant growth. It took many years, however, for the growth in student numbers to become established. Only since the Second World War has participation in university education increased explosively and at the same time the university's role as a research institution become more and more prominent. As a result of these developments, universities have become so large that they are starting to resemble businesses, meaning that they are often managed as such: one increasingly hears terms such as professional management, professional fundraising, valorization and efficiency. Hardly anyone would doubt that given the size of the budgets involved – in many cases, ranging from half a billion to one and a half billion euros – good, professional leadership is essential. But this same need for tighter and more efficient management is causing great dissatisfaction among many lecturers and students. Again, it is Stefan Collini who comprehensively expresses the oft-heard complaint that traditional academic freedom has largely disappeared and that valorization has come to the fore: 'universities have been transformed to the point where many are now principally centres of scientific and technological research and, increasingly, of vocational and professional training.[4] Although Collini enjoys much support within the academic community, such statements present the university as an otherworldly institution; one that is difficult to reconcile with the challenges facing the world, and one from which society is simply demanding visibility and commitment.

The dissatisfaction felt by Collini and many others becomes clearer, however, when we consider the fact that as a consequence of market demand, there is a danger that the research carried out by the 'entrepreneurial university' will shift unilaterally towards those areas where the greatest opportunities for valorization lie. Indeed, it is not difficult to show that since the Second World War and especially since 1980, the volume of research in the medical, biomedical and natural sciences has increased exponentially all over the world, often to the detriment of the humanities and social sciences. It is thus no surprise that these latter disciplines have been particularly harsh critics of the modern system: many pages of *The Guardian, The Economist, The New York Times, Trouw* and *NRC* have played host to scholars complaining about the lack of attention paid to the humanities, the liberal arts and sciences or the social sciences, in contrast to (from the perspective of those doing the complaining) the massive attention lavished on technology and the natural sciences. It is in this context that reference is often made to the ideas of Von Humboldt, and there are loud calls for universities to give more space to *Bildung*, without realizing that it was precisely the Humboldtian concept of the link between teaching and research that gave rise to the current situation in the first place.

The fourth and final major problem likewise shows how the university is wrestling with its modern identity. Rather than originating in the Enlightenment, this is a problem that has, according to the critics, become much more defined in recent decades, under pressure from the factory-like production of knowledge that changed the university beyond all recognition from the late 1980s onwards. For centuries, the university had a widely recognized duty to disseminate the knowledge that had been gathered. Scholarly treatises and publications are as old as the university itself, and served primarily to maintain an exchange of knowledge and above all, to record knowledge in a public archive. For hundreds of years, scholars published only in order to exchange knowledge and to establish their reputations; publication was hardly a commercial phenomenon. With the explosive global growth of the universities from the 1970s, however, the volume of research increased sharply. With this came rising demand for and a supply of publications, and what had previously hardly been a commercial market for scientific journals was rapidly commercialized. Whereas university publishers or learned societies, such as the Royal Society in England or the Royal Academy of Sciences in the Netherlands, had first served the market, large publishers assumed leadership of the professional organization of the whole process – for a fee, of course. The growth in publications was and still is explosive, but the university was only truly caught in its grip when publication output was measured on a constant basis. From that time onwards, a spiral of pressure to publish developed, and increasing costs for access to publications – publications that, ironically enough, were reporting the results of what was often publicly-financed research.[6,7]

The debate today

These four problems together form the main ingredients of the debate that is dominating the universities in different countries, to varying extents. In America, there is talk of

6   Dijstelbloem, H., F. Huisman, F. Miedema & W. Mijnhardt, 2013: '*Waarom de wetenschap niet werkt zoals het moet, en wat daaraan te doen is*'. Science in Transition, Position paper 2013. Critical argument about the mechanisms that lead to greater prioritization of quantity and production, and less prioritization of quality and content. See also http://www.scienceintransition.nl.
7   Wilsdon, J., et al., 2015: *The Metric Tide: Report of the Independent Review of the Role of Metrics in Research Assessment and Management.* DOI: 10.13140/ RG.2.1.4929.1363. HEFCE. Offers a useful overview of the background to metrics in academia and their effects.

the university in crisis, but in Europe, too, an increasing number of voices are claiming, often in vehement terms, that there is something wrong with the entire system. It is an international debate, in other words, with different emphases. Usually, though, it is about the tenability of old values and structures, and the question of whether these remain adequate in the twenty-first century. The debate also questions the core values of today's university; these, too, were largely inherited from another age, meaning that we also need to ask whether they are still relevant. Viewed the other way, it is often asked, especially in Europe, whether we should not take a step back from modern developments, and a case is made for a return to old values.

In addition to these themes, which touch on the past, there are also many questions about the future; about what the university will be like in the coming decades.[8] Although there are many common elements, this future seems very different in all of the countries and on the three continents of North America, Europe and Asia. *The* university does not exist and there are many differences in the national contexts. In the Netherlands, for example, the debate about the problems with which the university is grappling has been more intense than in many other countries. In the spring of 2015, riots broke out in Amsterdam, with students explicitly protesting the state of affairs within contemporary universities. They occupied important buildings on the University of Amsterdam campus for quite some time, along with buildings belonging to other universities in the Netherlands, as movements

8   Barnett, R., 2011: *Being a University*, Routledge, 188 pp. Wide-ranging study of the core values and objectives of the university. Older but still very readable is Boulton, G. & C. Lucas, 2008: '*What Are Universities For*', LERU position paper 2008.

emerged that came to be referred to under the banner of 'The New University'.[9]

Why have the general problems in the Netherlands come to light in a more vehement fashion? It seems that this is related to a convergence of international and national events. The discontent about the pressure to publish and the almost-autonomous conveyor-belt of research against which the 'Science in Transition' movement[6] in the Netherlands and comparable groups elsewhere are protesting, are widely recognisable phenomena at the international level, particularly in scientific and medical university departments. The complaints about valorization and the entrepreneurial university are also widely recognisable, now especially on the part of the social sciences and humanities. In the Netherlands, however, this broad international debate appears to have been put under further pressure by the performance agreements that the universities concluded with the government in 2012.[9] Agreements were made by the then Cabinet on numerous elements that, taken together, were meant to lead to a significant improvement in the quality of education. Due to their detailed nature, however, they severely curtailed universities' freedom. This, in any case, is what underlies the numerous complaints about 'output-driven thinking': the freedom is gone, and many believe that the university has degenerated into a teaching factory.[10]

9   Thomas, C., 2015: *Competente rebellen. Hoe de universiteit in opstand kwam tegen het marktdenken*, Amsterdam University Press, 213 pp.

10   Flikkema, M., (ed.), 2016: *Sense of Serving. Reconsidering the Role of Universities Now*, VU University Press, 184 pp. Critical reflection on the nature of modern university education in the Netherlands.

2.   A history of secularization and democratization

The university has an eight-hundred-year history, and many of the problems with which we are grappling today crept in during that long period. Some of these problems have become so self-evident that we no longer even know where they came from. Sometimes they concern major questions: why should scholarship be independent? Is it actually independent? But even very basic differences in understanding can confuse the discussion: does *the* university exist, or is the same word used on different continents to express totally different ideas? Although we do not make any distinction in our use of language, and speak of 'the university' as though that is all there is to it, the word conceals a wide range of possible models. *The* university does not exist: higher education has a long history, one that is different on every continent and that has led to different systems on each continent, each of which now faces its own problems.

An extensive debate is currently taking place in America, for example, that is largely about the role of government in higher education. In this respect, Michael Crow presents an interesting case. He is playing a prominent role in this debate and speaks with some frequency in committees of the United States Congress or government commissions. As the president of Arizona State University (ASU), he changed tack completely a decade or so ago. Instead of making his university more selective and elitist, he made the case for accessibility, interdisciplinarity and innovation. This idea also formed the basis for his book with

William Dabars,[1] in which he presents the ASU model as a solution to the American problem of rising tuition fees and increasingly limited access to good university education.

Many of the Ivy League universities, the top universities where members of the American elite study, view him as an alarmist know-it-all and accuse him of behaving like an adolescent, because he is always laying into established institutions. The fact is, though, that he has a vision of the whole system (one that is shared by the ex-president of New York University, John Sexton, among others),[2] which makes the core point that broad accessibility has been the key to success in American universities over the last fifty years. He sees more limited access as a result of rising financial barriers, combined with a certain lack of willingness to innovate, as the greatest threat to the 'Great American Research University'.

Crow and Dabars represent a progressive flank in the American debate, in the sense that on the one hand they are great supporters of the American system, but on the other hand, they sharply denounce the same system's problems in relation to governmental participation. In their book, they analyse the characteristics of what they call the 'most successful system in the world', tracing a direct line back from the emergence of the American universities, via the medieval European universities, to the Greek academies. This is striking, because the modern system is thereby implicitly bathed in the light of the Greek philosophers. This image recurs as an ideal in many modern debates: Plato's first Academy (named after Akademos, who owned the land on which the first school was built), the place where, following Plato and

1   Crow, Michael M. & William B. Dabars, 2015: *Designing the New American University*, Johns Hopkins University Press.
2   Sexton, J., 2014: *Access that Matters: Quality Education for All.* Unpublished address, November 2, 2014.

Aristotle, philosophy was taught to the citizens of Athens for many years. Whilst tracing American universities back to this entails making rather a large leap, Crow and Dabars rightly observe that the American system combines two successful elements that originate from earlier phases in the university's development: the college model with its broad education, as promoted by Newman, and the graduate phase in which teaching and research are combined in a manner that can be traced back to the ideas of Von Humboldt.

It is often claimed that it is this combination that makes the American system the most successful in the world. As evidence for this, Crow and Dabars simply point to the fact that many of the universities in the global top-50 are American and that modern research is dominated by successful American universities. The analysis is somewhat vague, however, when it comes to precisely what the drivers of this success have been. At first sight, it seems to have had more to do with the constant growth in the American economy after the great crisis of the 1920s, and with the accompanying prosperity that led to the enormous capitalization of American research, than the form of the system. In addition, the national culture of intense competition and stringent selection on the basis of talent has undoubtedly played a role. Nevertheless, when explaining America's success, American authors often emphasize the importance of the system and the way in which it is organized – that is, a broad college education in which the first years form the foundation for a specialized phase – as the explanation for this success. And this begs the question of what actually drives systems of higher education, what the main changes are over longer periods, and what the possible disruptive factors are that have led, or will lead, to rapid and fundamental changes.

The earliest history of the university

It is typically American to see the 'Great American Research University' as the pinnacle of a system that can be traced back directly to the Greek *akademeia*. This fails to do justice to the very diverse currents that led from Classical Antiquity to the university systems to be found on the different continents today.[3] These are shown schematically in Figure 1. After the fall of the Greek academies in the fourth century AD, the centre of gravity of higher education shifted first to Mesopotamia and later to Persia. These traditions partly preserved the character of Greek education, with many practical applications in technology and medicine, for example. The link with religion was always strong, though, meaning that access to education was limited: scholarship was an elite occupation. One should add that this was also true of the systems that developed in parallel in India, which produced very high-quality scholarship between 800 and 1400. It is striking that the Chinese system had a much less prominent profile in this period.

Within the Islamic tradition, there was great interest in learning from the outset, and the Greek inheritance

---

3   This part is based on a very wide range of literature. Among others, I consulted Ruegg (ed.), *A History of the University in Europe*, which gives an extensive overview of the European history from medieval times till the 20th century; see also https://en.wikipedia.org/wiki/University. Crow and Dabars (2015), who focus on the development of the American system. Furthermore: see, for example, Cohen, F., 2007: *De herschepping van de wereld*. The University of Salamanca has produced various publications that describe its history in detail. See also: https://en.wikipedia.org/wiki/University_of_Salamanca. In addition, see publications from the University of Bologna, and https://en.wikipedia.org/wiki/University_of_Bologna. On the history of science, a lot of accessible information can be found, for example, at https://en.wikipedia.org/wiki/History_of_science.

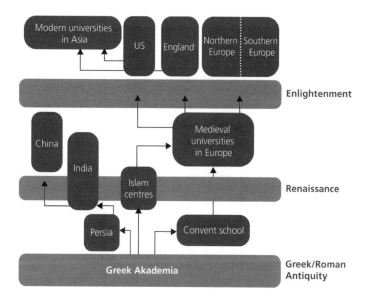

Fig. 1: Diagrammatical representation of the development of the systems on the different continents over time. The diagram shows the major effects of the Renaissance and the Enlightenment, but it also shows how a high level of differentiation emerged in the course of history.

played a major role. In centres of learning such as Cairo and Baghdad, important schools developed in the early Middle Ages that blended Greek knowledge with elements from the Persian and Indian systems. With the expansion of the Islamic sphere of influence, much of the knowledge that had been gathered was exported to other regions. Córdoba, for example, grew rapidly to become a centre of European scholarship and functioned as a source of inspiration for the oldest universities. In addition to these contacts with the Islamic world via for instance Spain and Sicily, the translations of the classics that were made in what was then Moorish Toledo, among other places, played a key role. The crusades, which initially disrupted the expansion of all of this knowledge to Europe, later proved to have been of enormous significance in opening it up. This formed the basis for the universities in the Middle Ages.

Until the founding of medieval universities, almost all forms of 'higher education' had a strongly religious character and access to them was limited. From 1200, this picture slowly changed in Europe: for the first time, educational institutions started to distance themselves from their religious foundations. It was no longer a system that was exclusively for the church and the feudal ruler; instead, it became more democratic and more widely accessible. In this sense, the rise of the medieval universities formed part of the new Renaissance approach to knowledge and beauty, but now not only at the feudal courts, but also in what were increasingly independent city states, particularly those that emerged early in Italy. It should thus come as no surprise that this was where the first universities flourished.

The broader and increasingly middle-class nature of university education was given huge impetus by the discovery of the art of printing. If the Renaissance, with its new climate of knowledge and the arts, had been a forceful undercurrent, the discovery of printing was what is known in modern jargon as a truly 'disruptive technology', and had a radically democratizing effect on the university world and the dissemination of knowledge. Knowledge no longer circulated in handwritten form mainly in monasteries and at the feudal courts, but became more and more widely available in printed form.

Despite all these changes, the character of the university appeared to remain the same for many years: it was only accessible to a relatively narrow section of the population, and much scholarship took place within the fields of theology, law, philosophy and medicine. Although there was gradual progress in the natural sciences, despite all the discoveries, science remained religiously inspired for many years. We forget all too easily that even Newton spent a large part of his time on what we would now call pure alchemy. Even the form of the university changed only slowly, and for many years it remained as the church had intended: focused not on the acquisition of new knowledge, but primarily on the preservation and transfer of old knowledge. Much of the teaching took place in colleges that strongly resembled the old monasteries in their form and house rules, a structure that has been most clearly preserved in universities such as Oxford and Cambridge, and that can still be found in North America as well.

From the outset, the university was a distinct institution with its own police force and own legal authorities and laws, despite the continuing links with the church and state. The University of Salamanca is a good example of these early developments. Founded in 1218 by King Alfonso IX, the university was granted a papal bull in 1255. King Alfonso X in particular left his mark on the university: known as El Sabio (the Wise), he established numerous regulations that led to the university's flourishing. He ensured that the students were able to get affordable food, and that the students were forbidden to carry arms, so as to prevent fights; and above all, he established the Magna Carta of Salamanca, a law that regulated both the subjects and the content of the education – there was no such thing as independent scholarship at that time!

There was an important saying in the University of Salamanca in those years: *Omnium Scientiarum Princeps Salmantica Docet* (Salamanca, foremost in the teaching of all the sciences). This referred emphatically to what was then the ideal of systematically teaching the whole body of scholarship in a broad and comprehensive way, rather than in a specialized fashion or with a view to a profession. This was supported by a curriculum that provided a thorough grounding in Greek and Latin, although one should note that languages were not held in high regard in Salamanca: the professors were badly paid and their chairs had little prestige. But this broad training – in what we now call the *literae humaniores* – was compulsory for everyone before they could choose a 'real' field.

In addition to languages, music, rhetoric, astronomy and even medicine were held in low esteem. By contrast, theology and all kinds of law were amply represented in Salamanca. From canon law to civil law, these were prominent chairs with their own enormous lecture halls: more than half of the halls around the old cloisters where the university was accommodated from 1415 were reserved for law. It should thus come as no surprise that this was where the elites of the Spanish Kingdom and later the Empire were trained; for centuries, almost the entire administrative and governmental staff of the Spanish kings and emperors came from Salamanca. This bond between *universitas* and state was much more limited elsewhere, however, where law had a lower status. In the somewhat younger Northern European universities, for example, primarily the arts and theology were held in high esteem, and for this reason alone, these universities played a lesser role in the state administration. This distinction between North and South is still discernible in Europe, because in general, the Southern European universities have a stronger tendency to prepare students for professional roles than those in Northern Europe.

From these first 'universities', which were often extremely small and generally did not even have their own accommodation, the university slowly took shape as an institution. The oldest university dates from 1088 (Bologna

University, declared autonomous by Emperor Frederick Barbarossa in 1158). More than four hundred years later, every large town had a university or illustrious school. With the expansion in numbers, the character of the university also changed: very slowly, also under the influence of the natural sciences, the emphasis shifted from preserving and transferring traditional knowledge to unlocking new knowledge, paired with cautious steps towards the further secularization of scholarship. Although the church continued to see the university as a guardian of ancient values, the latter increasingly developed its independent character.

Major changes since the Enlightenment

The character of the universities, which was then still essentially medieval, changed fundamentally during the Enlightenment: in this period, science and religion were separated for good and knowledge acquired new meaning as a result of the new striving for objectivity, free from ecclesiastical morals and secular norms. This typically Romantic conception of independent, non-normative scholarship expanded rapidly and continues to influence the debate today. In the nineteenth century, it gave a new impetus to the development of the universities. The idea of *Bildung* played a key role in this, and it is odd that this concept is still largely attributed to Von Humboldt alone. Grounded in Enlightenment ideals, it was an idea that enjoyed relatively widespread support and had already spread rapidly. Von Humboldt's great contribution was to take the ideal of *Bildung* a major step further. As the Prussian education minister, he prescribed that research should be linked to teaching in all universities, and that students should receive systematic training in how to do ᵕood research. Indeed, he argued painstakingly that this should be the distinguishing characteristic of the university in comparison with all other forms of education. And it was in this – in institutionalizing an ideal – that Von Humboldt proved to be utterly innovative. From that time onwards, the role of the university changed fundamentally: from being a guardian and conveyor of knowledge, the university became the place where new knowledge was discovered and, moreover, where students were trained to do this. This idea proved to be very influential; in the US (at Harvard, for example) relatively early in the nineteenth century, it led to the introduction of a graduate phase in which teaching and research were linked, following on from a broad, formative undergraduate phase. The American model of the research university was born.[4]

At the beginning of the nineteenth century, Napoleon implemented significant reforms across all of Europe, or at least in those parts of the continent where he was in power. The effects of this are still visible today, in spite of the changes that were introduced within the European Union at the end of the 20th century: the Scandinavian countries and Germany have a different system of higher education than the Netherlands, Belgium and France do, for example. The English university system sidestepped the general reforms that Napoleon implemented. This means that in addition to the differences between Northern and Southern European

4   Crow and Dabars (2015) offer a concise overview of the development of the American system. See also *Beyond the University* by Roth (2014), and Bok (2013): *Higher Education in America*. See also: '*Science, The Endless Frontier*. A Report to the President by Vannevar Bush, Director of the Office of Scientific Research and Development, July 1945'. This latter report gave a great boost to government investment in the universities, and thereby scholarly production in North America and later Europe. The report is grounded in a deeply rooted belief in scholarship as a social force.

universities, there are also major differences between these and universities in the United Kingdom. Mainly in the nineteenth and twentieth centuries, the Anglo-Saxon model of the university spread from England and later from America to Asia, where universities with very different forms were deeply rooted in local and longstanding traditions.

A motley system thus took shape, with significant differences between Anglo-Saxon and European countries. While these countries are experiencing their own problems, they have also inherited common features, such as the idea of independent scholarship, the interweaving of teaching and research, and the principle of free access. And in fact, from the time of the expansion of the modern university in the mid-nineteenth century, prosperity played a major role in driving the size and expansion of the university system. Governments increasingly saw higher education as a tool for realizing state objectives through having a well-educated population, and with the gradual rise in prosperity from 1850 until around 1980, there was almost continuous investment in higher education in both the old and the new worlds.

A 1945 report by Vannevar Bush (the director of the American Office of Scientific Research and Development), commissioned by President Roosevelt, would give a particular boost to the university system and have a global impact. Bush wrote in his report:

> Basic scientific research is scientific capital. Moreover, we cannot any longer depend upon Europe as a major source of this scientific capital. Clearly, more and better scientific research is one essential to the achievement of our goal of full employment. How do we increase this scientific capital? First, we must have plenty of men and women trained in science, for upon them depends both the creation of new knowledge

and its application to practical purposes. Second, we must strengthen the centers of basic research which are principally the colleges, universities, and research institutes.[4]

One is struck by the precision with which Bush formulated the objectives of science: to fight disease, for (national) security and for public welfare. Bush was setting out a scientific politics that linked, in a flexible way, fundamental research to the objectives of the government, with the latter explicitly presented as the patron of 'basic research'. From that time, there was much less debate in North America about the ties between the government, industry and research than in Europe, where the idea of the entrepreneurial university still gives rise to problems today.

The problems are deeply asymmetrical in another respect. Thanks to growing prosperity, mainly from the 1970s onwards, the democratization of the university – which was already underway – assumed the character of free access. In the Netherlands, this was captured in the slogan 'education for the many [*onderwijs voor velen*]'. Almost everywhere, wider participation in higher education became part of national political policy. It quickly became clear, however, that due to this expansion, the system threatened to become a victim of its own success. In North America and Europe, investment per student dropped significantly from 1990; a fall that was accentuated by the successive financial crises after 2002, faltering economic growth and rapidly expanding national health budgets. Although there was (and still is) strong growth in demand for university education in both Europe and North America, governments responded to this in different ways. In North America and, to a lesser extent, in England, the state withdrew further than in Europe. As a result, the costs for students have exploded in Anglo-Saxon countries and rising tuition fees have become a growing problem. Thus, while access to university education may seem to have been democratized after many centuries, this is largely the case for the financially better-off.

It is this mass influx into the university that lies at the root of almost all the problems that universities are currently facing. This is also an important 'button' that the government and the university could press: stemming the huge inflow of students could make a real contribution to solving today's problems. It must be borne in mind in this context that, in virtually all of Western Europe, access to higher education is seen as a right that must be guaranteed by government, provided, of course, that prospective students have obtained the relevant qualifications that are required. In general, selective admission is considered something to be avoided, and it only takes place on a fairly limited scale. However, the belief that access to higher education is a universal right goes much further than that: in many cases, tuition fees in Europe are extremely low, and in a number of countries, such as Sweden and Germany, many people argue that higher education should remain completely free. This 'socialist' view of higher education contrasts quite starkly with the Anglo-Saxon attitude, which also prevails in Asia. Here, selective admission is seen as essential in order to guarantee first-rate quality, and the higher-education landscape is ruled much more by the user-pays principle than is the case in Northwestern Europe. But in spite of these differences in views, there are many arguments in favour of shifting towards the expanded use of selective admission processes in the European context. This would be a radical decision, though, with major political and societal implications, and we shall thus return to the dilemma of selection vs. free access in the following chapters.

3.   Grappling with change

The great expansion in student numbers began in the mid-nineteenth century, driven by the gradual rise in prosperity. It was the massive influx in the second half of the twentieth century, however, that led to the exponential growth of the universities that lies at the root of many of today's problems. It is interesting to examine how this is being tackled, in order to gain a better understanding of the university's capacity for change. For on the one hand, there are loud calls for a return to fundamental tasks such as teaching, and administrators are being reproached for failing to solve problems properly; and on the other hand, it is questionable whether the university can indeed determine its own course in this respect. Perhaps the external forces are so formidable that the university is largely a plaything of events, and is being forced into unavoidable or even undesirable decisions.

In recent decades, all Western countries experienced an abrupt change in the peaceful and seemingly automatic manner in which government funding kept pace with growth. This was caused by the relative contraction of government resources, mainly due to the rising cost of public healthcare. Governments are now paying considerably less per student, and universities have only two or three options available to make up for this fall in funding. In the first place, they can increase tuition fees, to set off the fall in income with a rising contribution from the user, the student. In recent decades, this option has been used mainly in the US and England. A second way is via valorization, that is to say, providing knowledge in exchange for funding from societal partners; and a third way is via gifts and donations.

Not only do these shifting funding flows have major implications for the university, but they also touch directly on the fundamental question of whether university education should be financed from public or private funds, which naturally also raises the issue of autonomy. He who pays the piper calls the tune; if the state makes a significant contribution, as in Northwestern Europe, in many cases it often demands a considerable say in how the institutions are run in return. To put it the opposite way, if the state withdraws, institutions gain more autonomy, in the last resort becoming entirely private institutions that operate separately from the state. This is therefore the first dilemma that modern universities are facing: there are more universities than ever before, they are better than ever, and across the world, governments maintain that having a highly-educated population is a mainstay of policy. At the same time, however, particularly in Anglo-Saxon countries and to a lesser extent in Europe as well, government funding is falling and an increasingly privatized system threatens to emerge, with less accessibility owing to the selection that comes with it.

On the whole, universities are behaving quite passively in the face of this dilemma. There is a tendency to raise potential problems by referring plaintively to the government's obligation to make up budget shortfalls. In Anglo-Saxon countries, by contrast, there are universities that can sense opportunities here and are increasingly operating in a private market. But virtually nowhere is an open debate being held to explore the chances and opportunities that are flowing from the new situation, or the great risks posed by a growing social divide, such as those that come with following the path of least resistance; namely, that of privatization.

The massive growth of the university

After the Second World War, participation in higher education increased significantly in all OECD countries, driven by government policy. This not only resulted in the accessibility-related problems described above, but it also had an impact on the institutions themselves. In that fifty-year period, the universities grew by around a factor of ten,[1] if one includes the accompanying expansion in support processes, the management of financial flows and buildings. Universities have become businesses for which efficiency is just as important as it is for industry, certainly given the drop in funding. It is no coincidence that there have been complaints all around the world about the 'managers' who have taken over the university from lecturers and students.

This second problem also calls for far-reaching decisions, but the question is whether the university is able to make these freely. The problem mainly seems to be affecting universities in continental Europe, where there is no selection and regulating growth is therefore proving difficult. In this respect, too, it is necessary to have an active debate about selection and its consequences. At the same time, however, there is a need for greater balance in the debate about size. It is unacceptable that the gulf here between administrators on the one hand, and lecturers and students on the other, threatens to become even wider. All parties will have to search for solutions. The situation is not aided by what is often the great distrust with which university administrators are viewed when they strive for efficiency and the optimal use of resources. Viewed the other way, administrators are taking refuge in an ever-growing stack

---

[1]   Working Papers OESO, 2012: *'Educational Attainments OECD, 1960-2010'.*

of regulations in an attempt to keep the size of universities manageable, and they often pay strikingly little attention to the conditions of relative freedom in which the university best thrives.

A third problem where the modern university faces deadlock is also related to shifting funding flows. The concept of valorization has made its appearance everywhere; it arrived in the Netherlands early, under the motto of 'the entrepreneurial university'. The consequences are evident and sometimes far-reaching. In the first place, the shift in funding is undoubtedly having an effect on the type of research done, with a shift from so-called blue-sky or curiosity-driven (fundamental) research to applied research. Many researchers perceive this inevitable steering of research, as well as its commercial and often limited basis, as an encroachment on academic freedom. Here, too, people are quick to blame the management culture and the dominance of financial backers from industry, but at the same time, it is widely recognized that valorization is a financial necessity. And not only financial, for many of those who criticize valorization also think that the university should have a permanent, visible presence in society; and participation in privately-financed projects that tackle what are evidently socially significant problems is undoubtedly one relevant way of doing this.

The changing role of government and the new arrangements for conducting research forms part of the neoliberal course known as the 'New Public Management', which made its entrance after the Reagan-Thatcher era of the 1980s. As result of globalization, its effects can be seen everywhere in the global convergence of systems of higher education. Unlike in America and Asia, where collaboration with industry is much more acceptable and where are even justifiable warnings about the excessive influence of the private sector on the independence of research, in Europe universities feel relatively little urgency to make societal contributions such as these. Although there could be a debate about the university's duty, among others, to boost innovation and the economy, what we often see instead is an appeal for independent and free scholarship. But too little resistance is being shown in this debate, in the sense that the one does not necessarily exclude the other; indeed, it is essential that the university reconsider its role in this respect.

As early as the 1990s, a group of scholars led by Helga Nowotny argued for a reconsideration of the inflexible view that scholarship should be financed by society and that the latter should then wait to see what it would get in return.[2] In the group's opinion, this so-called 'Mode 1' form of scholarship should be transformed into 'Mode 2': knowledge should be produced in interdisciplinary contexts in the service of specific societal problems and issues. The fact that as president of the European Research Council (ERC), Nowotny mainly funded 'Mode 1' programmes says a lot about the difficulty of effecting change in academia.

Finally, there is a fourth problem, which in essence is also a consequence of the great success that higher education has enjoyed, and that is increasingly becoming symbolic of the problems facing the modern university. From the Second World War onwards, not only did participation in the university system rise dramatically, but also the universities themselves, including the accompanying research, grew to be many times larger. The production of scientific research,

2   Gibbons, M., C. Limoges, H. Nowotny, S. Schwartzman, P. Scott & M. Trow, 1994: *The New Production of Knowledge: The Dynamics of Science and Research in Contemporary Societies*, Sage.

measured on the basis of the number of publications, has correspondingly expanded to unprecedented levels and is still growing. In principle, there is nothing wrong with this, but this problem has also gradually become unmanageable due to the explosive nature of the growth. As a result, many publications are not, or hardly, read, and much research is not or hardly cited. The financial importance of publishing as a means of making researchers and institutions visible has become so great, however, that it is not easy for the university to reverse this spiral.

An accumulation of problems

The high value accrued by publications as a way to establish reputations means that with the huge growth in output and the number of researchers, publishing has become a mega-business, particularly since the 1970s. Publishing firms are earning large sums from publishing journals and books, which entails taking over the researchers' intellectual property and making it available for a fee. Although services are provided in return, varying from arranging the peer review process to printing articles or publishing them online, universities and researchers are no longer de facto in charge of their own research results. Competition between researchers and institutions for the available funds is an extremely important, if not the only, factor in this process. Almost every university takes part in rewarding employees' publications, whereby they make a key contribution to preserving the system. Universities have become the prisoners of the league tables that compare them to one another, and they are loath to abandon them unilaterally for fear of the consequences. The universities have been sucked, step by step, into a system from which they are now hardly able to extract themselves.

The spiral of attaching ever-more importance to research is inevitably taking its toll in the form of increasing pressure on other tasks, especially teaching. This has become a particular problem in university departments that have traditionally put a strong emphasis on teaching, such as the humanities and social sciences. What is playing a role here is not only the magnitude of the task, but also, and perhaps even more so, the fact that research is valued so much more highly than teaching. As a result, a deeply-felt pecking order has emerged across the globe, one that is causing much discontent: a division between 'rich' fields with lots of research funding and space for teaching, such as the natural, medical and technical sciences, and 'poor' fields such as the humanities and social sciences – with every possible gradation of discontent between the two extremes.

In itself, each of the four dilemmas identified so far in this chapter has major implications for the functioning of the modern university. In combination, however, they have produced a system that is under serious pressure; pressure so great that it is clear that unless a new course is taken, there will be a crisis – and in the US in particular, a crisis no longer seems a distant possibility. In that country, the knock-on effects are already visible in the form of sky-high tuition fees and major societal dissatisfaction with the whole system. One could ask whether this even means that an institution that has managed to survive and move with the times for the past eight hundred years might go the way of many other institutions that have buckled in recent decades; think of the changes that have occurred in financial institutions, the legal system and government. All of these institutions have lost authority and recognition, and the university may suffer the same fate if solutions are not found to the abovementioned problems.

All of the problems that have been described appear to be global problems to a greater or lesser extent, despite the fact that government strategies differ by country. Thus, much more than national political decision-making, the fate of the university appears to be determined by major societal phenomena. The root cause of many of the problems identified above is growing participation in higher education and, with this, the explosive growth in student numbers worldwide. But it is precisely on this point that governments may perceive more potential for change than on others, for the state can make a crucial choice here: it can step back and leave selective access 'to the market', or it can facilitate wide access to higher education by making a substantial contribution to its financing. In the first case, we see the rise of a highly-privatized system such as that in the US, where student access is determined by income and talent. In the second case, we get a broad system like the one in Northwestern Europe, where free access to what is predominantly a public system is mainly determined by a certain minimal level of quality on the part of the student, and parental income plays a relatively minor role. It is on this point that the government's role is crucial: access for a small elite to the top universities, accompanied by inevitable and growing social division; or broad access to a system with little differentiation and fewer top universities, but more social cohesion. We will consider this contrast in more detail in the next chapter.

Over the past thirty years, universities around the world, particularly those in North America and Europe, have come under heavy pressure. Looking back, we can see that universities have tended to be affected by the changes, rather than choosing their own course; there has been very little resistance or steering. The pressure of societal change forced the university out of its ivory tower, the university even became an entrepreneurial institution, it became an institution of mass education – all without there having been any counteraction. Aside from the period around 1968, when students rebelled against old-fashioned university governance, the university as a whole has hardly mounted the barricades in order to defend itself against all the developments. Whilst movements such as 'Science in Transition' and 'the New University' are certainly protesting, and in the Netherlands there were occupations in Amsterdam in 2015, the debate remains limited. Why is this the case?

We must conclude that the university has lost authority and is exercising less and less influence in the societal and political debate. As such, it is increasingly becoming the plaything of major social currents. However, one hardly finds any close internal communities within universities that adopt a tough joint stance on the developments that they consider undesirable. This means that there are very few collectively-held conceptions of what the university should be, on which joint action could be based.[3] In short: the university has become a normal enterprise, an institution that delivers services. This is dangerous, because from this position the university is more like a ship being buffeted by the waves of time than a ship that is setting a firm course towards a new future.

3   Barnett, R., 2011: *Being a University*, Routledge, 188 pp.

4.   Rising costs, selection and governments in retreat

Higher education is a hot topic in the US: newspapers such as *The New York Times*[1] devote long articles in weekend supplements to the rising costs, the sharply rising levels of student debt, and, above all, access to higher education. In June 2015, readers were even invited to estimate what percentage of each income category of the population had access to university at that time. A few days later, the newspaper published the results, which showed that many readers – according to their answers – were unduly pessimistic about reality; of the very lowest income categories, 15% had access, whilst the majority of readers had estimated 0%! That estimate alone was already revealing... The somewhat more positive picture was spoiled, however, when the newspaper added that whilst 15% had been admitted, the percentage of drop-outs in this group was extremely high, much higher than among students from better social backgrounds. *The New York Times* thus concluded that social background is winning over talent: to be poor and talented is clearly not a successful combination in the American system.

Although political party programmes would suggest otherwise, in parts of Western Europe and the Netherlands, just as in America, one finds a deeply-rooted trend towards less willingness on the part of the state to invest in higher education. This is partly the result of budgetary factors, such as the rising costs of healthcare, but in the US there is a significant group

---

1   Dynarski, S., 2015: '*For the Poor, the Graduation Gap is Even Wider Than the Enrollment Gap*'. June 2, The New York Times.

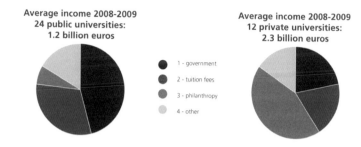

Fig. 2: Comparison of the size and composition of the incomes of public and private universities in the US. The average income of the private universities is twice that of the public universities, which is mainly due to income derived from endowments (private donations). Although it is difficult to make a comparison, private universities in the US have roughly four times more funding than comparably sized Dutch research universities. (Data derived from Lacroix and Maheu, 2015)

of politicians that emphatically considers state withdrawal desirable on principled grounds. From the mid-1980s, and accelerating in the first decade of the twenty-first century, state investment in the US fell, not only per student, but also in absolute terms: Lacroix and Maheu[2] find a fall of 25% between 1980 and 2000. Crow and Dabars[3] also paint a rather staggering picture of retrenchment by American governments, which started in the 1980s and only accelerated after the financial crisis of 2008. In the period between 2008 and 2013 alone, eleven states cut their higher education budgets by a third, and in Arizona and New Hampshire, budgets were halved in this period! When one adds the fall in gifts and donations and in investment from industry as a consequence of the financial crisis, an average picture emerges of sharply falling university incomes in recent years.

2   Lacroix, R. & L. Maheu, 2015: *Leading Research Universities in a Competitive World*, McGill Queen's University Press. Well-documented comparison of research universities in four countries, including insights into differences in funding.
3   Crow, Michael M. & William B. Dabars, 2015: *Designing the New American University*, Johns Hopkins University Press.

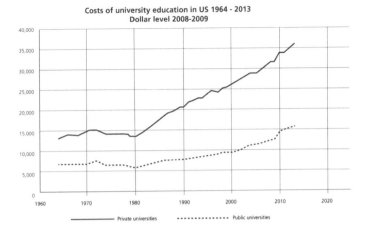

Fig. 3: Historical development of the cost of university education in the US based on the combined total of tuition fees and accommodation/food. The figure shows the rising costs and the increasing gap between public and private education. (Data: National Center for Education Statistics)

Figures 2 and 3 illustrate the differences in income and cost between the public and private universities. In the US, the financing of university education is a matter for the 51 states, which in recent years have given universities the freedom to raise tuition fees in tacit exchange for cuts in funding. And this has happened on a massive scale, certainly when it comes to the fees for out-of-state and international students. Moreover, the fees that are now being charged by the public universities are not so different from those charged by the private universities. This is rightly seen[4] as part of a trend towards the further privatization of education as the state simultaneously retreats.

4   Geiger, R.I., 2011: 'The Ten Generations of American Higher Education'. Higher Education in the Twenty-First Century: Social, Political and Economic Challenges. Altbach, P.G., P.J. Gumport & R.O. Berdahl (eds), Johns Hopkins University Press, 237-68.

All of the analyses agree that this spiral of government disinvestment, compensated by rapidly rising tuition fees, is undermining the whole system of higher education in the US. In addition to these two primary factors, there are three other factors in play that are sometimes interconnected: the weak economy, resulting in falling private income for the universities; the rise of private universities; and the digitization of teaching. Although all of these factors are weighed differently by different analysts, there is agreement on the combined effect: a deep-rooted division has emerged in the American system of higher education, with a small, rich, very selective top-layer of private institutions that are increasingly moving away from a increasingly bad, much less selective, second class of what are often public universities. If one adds the reports by *The New York Times*, a picture builds up of a limited number of elite universities for the rich, and a mass of badly functioning (largely public) universities for the poorer social classes.

As mentioned above, Michael Crow is one of the fiercest opponents and public critics of this system. He points to the catastrophic consequences of this divide, which will have a deep impact on society. He also points to the loss of talent, due to the fact that rates of participation in higher education among talented poor people are very low, and pleads for a far-reaching reversal of the trend towards government withdrawal. Like many others,[5,6] he is arguing for an increase in investment by the states and federal government.

---

5   National Academy of Sciences, 2015: *Research Universities and the Future of America. Ten Breakthrough Actions Vital to Our Nation's Prosperity and Security.* The National Academies Press. See also Bok (2013): *Higher Education in America* for an extensive overview of the American system and the problems it faces.
6   Sexton, J., 2014: *Access that Matters: Quality Education for All.* Unpublished address, November 2, 2014.

The great risks of privatization

On closer inspection, the situation is not as simple as Crow suggests, and it is questionable whether the trend towards dichotomy and privatization could still easily be reversed. On average, tuition fees already covered 43% of university budgets in 2006 (compared to 20% in 1980!). The universities have made full use of the freedom they were given by the states to plug the holes in their budgets by raising tuition fees, and they cannot afford to lose this income now. But with the withdrawal of the government, the latter has simultaneously divested itself of competencies:[7] both its responsibility to provide public facilities and its responsibility to regulate the market have been eroded, weakening the government's societal role. Due to the high level of autonomy of the universities, certainly the private ones, the government simply lacks the power and authority to steer effectively, and it will thus be difficult to make the system affordable and widely accessible again in the near future.

The inequality of opportunity in education is being felt increasingly widely as a reflection of the deep societal gulf between rich and poor. This gulf is becoming more evident in the US and will unavoidably lead to great social unrest: it was no coincidence that in 2013, President Obama spoke of the 'the nagging feeling among the poor and middle class that the deck is stacked against them'. It is patently obvious that the current system is unsustainable, provoking many calls to lower tuition fees and raise the government's

---

7   Lacroix, R. & L. Maheu, 2015: *Leading Research Universities in a Competitive World.* McGill-Queen's University Press. Provides a good discussion on the relationship between government control and funding when comparing the US and Canada, and the risks of having too little government participation.

contribution.[8] But what would an acceptable level of tuition fees be? Strikingly robust standpoints are taken on this in the American context. Sexton, among others, but also Lacroix and Maheu,[9] argue that students should see tuition fees and study costs as an investment in their future. Sexton even asserts that despite the enormous increase in tuition fees in recent years, the payback period of this investment has fallen and the fees are therefore still reasonable. *The Economist*[10] has also calculated that it still pays to invest in a university degree in the US, certainly if it is one from Harvard or another top university: in that case, the time needed to repay the debt falls dramatically due to the high salaries that can be commanded after graduating successfully.

Whilst much of the literature uses the profit principle to legitimize the cost of studying, the system is no longer considered stable if tuition fees have to cover more than 30% of the total university budget.[11] From this perspective, the comparison between Canada and the US is interesting, because the Canadian government has kept a considerably tighter hold on the system by investing in education. In Canada, the governmental contribution lies comfortably above 30%, and as a result, according to Lacroix and Maheu, the Canadian

8   Sexton, J., 2014: *Access that Matters: Quality Education for All.* Unpublished address, November 2, 2014.
9   Lacroix, R. & L. Maheu, 2015: *Leading Research Universities in a Competitive World.* McGill-Queen's University Press. The authors compare tuition fees in four countries and suggest that the relationship between the money spent and the payback time remains relatively favourable, even in Anglo-Saxon countries.
10   *The Economist*, 2015: 'Excellence v Equity'. Special Report Universities, March 28, 2015.
11   Lacroix, R. & L. Maheu, 2015: *Leading Research Universities in a Competitive World.* McGill-Queen's University Press. Here the 30%-norm is identified as a kind of empirical limit that is revealed by a comparison between the US and Canada, whereby in comparison to the US, the Canadian government has retained enough say to be able to prioritize accessibility and quality.

system faces many fewer problems than the American one. For the US, the way back seems virtually impassable: applying the 30% rule, most American universities would have to reduce tuition fees drastically, but this would mean that the lost income could only be compensated by the government: the income from endowments and other sources has levelled off too much in recent years to make up for the drop. Aside from the government's unwillingness to invest more, however, this is not something that the rich private institutions would want: after all, public funding would bring government regulation and a loss of independence. Why would they accept this? And there are still more than enough financially well-off students who are prepared to pay the high tuition fees.

The crucial question is thus where state participation should end and where the profit principle should begin, certainly when one bears in mind that the European universities still have a lot of room to raise tuition fees, an option that has been more or less maximized in the US and England. The realization that once this road has been taken, it is not easy to return, should cause European and Asian governments and universities to tread cautiously when responding to the pressure to replace government financing with higher tuition fees. Despite this, raising tuition fees in European universities is an option that governments will undoubtedly want to utilize, also in order to improve the quality of teaching and research. For a Dutch university such as Utrecht University, this would mean that if the government were to lower its contribution to 30% of the financing, compensation in the form of student payments would mean tuition fees of around 8,000 euros per year. In the European context, this is a shockingly high amount, which makes sense when you consider the fact that the Netherlands, with tuition fees of almost €2,000 per year, is among the more expensive places to study in North Western Europe. In American eyes, that would be a bargain; you invest in your future and the payback time is less than ten years, in most cases. For the university, however, it would add up to 180 million euros a year of latitude to improve quality, or otherwise to compensate for falling government contributions.

In the backwash of rising tuition fees, universities across the world are experiencing two additional problems that threaten the system over time. First of all, the private for-profit providers that now own 26% of all universities and colleges in the US.[12] Whilst they often perform badly and drop-out rates are high, their tuition fees are considerably lower than those of the selective universities. A well-known example is the University of Phoenix, with half a million students. Such universities do not have expensive buildings or do costly research, and are thus very competitive in certain educational sectors compared with classical universities. A second response to higher costs, which often goes hand in hand with private education, is the rise of digital teaching as a cheaper alternative. This has expanded rapidly over the last ten years, although its success remains limited and recognition of the modules of massive open online courses (MOOCs) in terms of degrees is still small. We should pay attention, however: recently, Arizona State University (ASU) was the first large university to recognise MOOCs (admittedly ASU's MOOCs, not those of a competitor) as part of the normal curriculum, and significant growth in digitization seems inevitable.

Why the American example is not one to follow

In view of all these problems, it should come as no surprise that many symposia, books and newspaper articles have been devoted to the 'Future of the American Research University'. The rich, strong, selective universities will easily survive the growing crisis and are therefore downplaying the threats. A university such as Harvard is mainly concerned about the federal financing of research and the flow of gifts, which in terms of volume are both dependent on the state of the economy and will be decisive for its success or failure. From his non-Ivy League university, however, John Sexton[8] has very clearly identified the social risks of increasingly inadequate access to good university education and the deepening societal divide that will result from this. He makes the case for a variegated system in which students are optimally placed via adequate selection and matching: someone with a lot of talent must have access to the best education, otherwise talent will be wasted and American education will lose what has long been its key advantage: a large population that is educated on the basis of talent, not on the basis of income. Strikingly, all of the analyses point to the enormous contribution that having a good system of higher education has made to American prosperity; the fear is that this basis will be lost and America will find itself in a backwater. Indeed, Sexton points to the current reversal in the flow of talent: no longer from Asia and Europe to the US, but the other way round. But a source as unimpeachable as the National Research Council has also pointed soberly to the danger that the landscape of higher education will change immensely in the coming years, and, with this, America will lose its leading position.[12] Van der Wende[13] shows that there will be a decrease in the brain drain of

12   King, G. & M. Sen, 2013: 'The Troubled Future of Colleges and Universities', *Political Science and Politics*, 46, 81-113.

13   Van der Wende, Marijk, 2015: 'International Academic Mobility: Towards a Concentration of the Minds in Europe'. *The European Review*, 23, 70-88

talent to the US, which may be further boosted by the outcome of the elections. Following the election of President Trump in late 2016, interest in Canadian universities increased by the factor of 10, at least judging by the number of visitors to the websites of Canada's top universities.[14]

It is not only in the US that cuts in government funding have put great pressure on the university system. In England as well, tuition fees have risen dramatically in recent years. In other European countries, too, and also in Asia in the coming period, this will become a significant bottleneck. But events in the US in recent decades teach us that a fall in the state's share of funding below a certain threshold leads to an almost irreversible spiral of rising tuition fees, actual privatization and narrowing access to the system, producing a sharply divided system consisting of a very small number of private top universities and a much broader system of what are on average mediocre public universities. This makes the case for government continuing to make a minimum contribution, whereby it could guarantee a high-quality Bachelor's phase, for example, so that wide access could be secured for this foundational phase in any case.

All over the world, a debate is being held about the role of government, which is slowly but surely being reduced certainly in the US and Europe. The Netherlands is a good example of how the debate on this topic tends to take place in a surprisingly covert way, with the government rarely stating openly that it is forced to, or seeks to, divest. For example, there has been a great deal of public discussion about the reforms to the relatively generous student

14 *Times Higher Education*, 2016: 'Trump Election Sparks Increased Interest in Canadian Universities'. November 2016.

grants system. In this, the students' unions – the Landelijk Studentenvakbond (LSvB) and the Interstedelijk Studenten Overleg (ISO) – have operated on the basis that students are being deprived of funds to which they are rightfully entitled. The government, on the other hand, points to its lack of financial leeway, which is comparable to that in other countries, and which will necessitate reforms to what are unsustainably high levels of financing over time. Finally, the universities hope that the funds that have been taken from the student grants system will eventually be made available again and added to their income. However, all of the parties are paying far too little attention to the fact that with the changed system of funding and, for example, the government's additional plans to raise tuition fees so that it can reduce its contribution, the fundamental issue of the privatization of education is looming ever closer.

It is not inconceivable that Western Europe will also follow the road taken in the US and, to a lesser extent, in England. This immediately raises the question of broad access to higher education. In these countries, limited access has resulted in a widening social dichotomy, and in the long term this will certainly lead to major problems. For this reason alone, the governments should strive to maintain wide access. But with this comes the important question of whether all students should go to a research university. At present, many students opt for university rather than higher vocational education for reasons of status and labour market prospects, rather than because they want a genuinely academic education. Indeed, in retrospect many students say that they had the wrong expectations when they started their training,[15] and it is thought that the high proportion of drop-outs[15,16] is due to the abstract nature of the course and the research skills that are by nature demanded by research-intensive universities, among other things.

In view of the interests at stake, it would be beneficial to hold this debate in Europe in much more clearly-defined terms than is now the case. Why not encourage more students to enter higher vocational education, which should naturally receive more money for this, and admit many fewer students to the research university, from which many quit, disappointed, after some time? From a financial perspective, it would be possible to strengthen higher professional education if considerably fewer students were to attend the expensive universities. This would allow us to guarantee the quality of both forms of higher education, and at the same time it would increase the affordability and accessibility of these institutions.

15   ResearchNed, 2015: *'Monitor beleidsmaatregelen 2015. Studiekeuze, studiegedrag, en leengedrag in relatie tot beleidsmaatregelen in het hoger onderwijs 2006-2015'.* Provides a detailed analysis on the extent of and reasons for student drop-out.
16   VSNU, 2012: *'Prestaties in perspectief. Trendrapportage universiteiten 2000-2020'.* Provides quantitative information on numerous aspects of funding and the quality of university education in the Netherlands.

5. On size, bureaucracy and distrust

Across the world, there is growing distrust within universities and an increasing gulf between students, lecturers and administrators. The core of this seems to lie in two phenomena at completely different levels. The first is institutional and concerns the question of ownership: to whom does the university actually belong? The second plays out at the level of the individual and is a question with which everyone in a large organization wrestles, namely: 'Am I still visible and valued?' Identifying with the modern university is evidently much more difficult than in the past, when everyone could find their place easily in compact, clearly structured universities.

Due to their large sizes and the large budgets that go with them, modern universities are increasing being managed as though they were large businesses – which they are, in many respects. Figures 4 and 5 illustrate the growth in the number of students and the relative fall in government funding in the Netherlands, a picture that is typical for Europe and North America. In recent decades, the growth in student numbers, the high degree of state withdrawal in some countries and the need to tap into other sources of funding have led to a fundamental change in the way in which universities are managed. But in many respects, this trend is utterly at odds with the nature of the university that developed from the Middle Ages onwards, characterized by the far-reaching autonomy of lecturers and researchers in relation to the institution, and the independence of the institution in relation to third parties. This independence

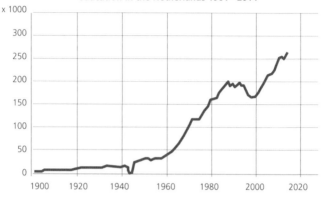

Fig. 4: Student participation in university education in the Netherlands, 1901-2014. The figure shows the explosive growth in the number of students since 1960, a phenomenon that can also be seen almost everywhere in Europe and the US. (Source: CBS)

was made possible, for example, by a mandate granted by the state or church with accompanying funding.

Everywhere else in the world, universities have likewise expanded massively since the Second World War, and for a significant number of universities and countries this growth has by no means reached its peak. The growth in Asia and South America has been exponential; it has happened to a lesser degree in Africa, but it will certainly come; and only in Europe and North America is growth levelling off. Demographically, this latter phenomenon is due to the ageing of these continents, which was for a long time compensated by increasing participation in higher education. And all over the world, growth was and still is being paired with the need to professionalize management and with increased accountability, whereby governments require ever more detailed justifications for the continuously growing volume of funding.

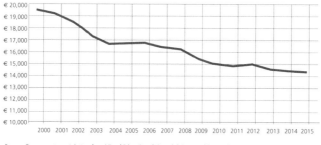

Government grant per student, 2000 - 2015, price level 2015
Including performance premiums

Source: Government grant: letters from Min of Education, Culture & Science and Economic
Affairs. Students: VSNU/CBS, 1cHO2015
Price indices: CPB/Macro Economische Verkenningen   *Graph produced by VSNU*

*Fig. 5: Fall in the state contribution per student in the Netherlands during the period
between 2000 and 2015, mainly caused by the growing number of students and the
failure of funding to keep up with this, even when so-called 'performance funding'
(a bonus for good performance) is taken into account. (Source: VSNU)*

It is clear that a university's size also determines the need
for professional management. But is this inevitably at odds
with the autonomy of the employees? And is there an optimal
size, whereby economies of scale still work and efficiency
advantages can be achieved, but the autonomy of lecturers
and students is preserved as far as possible? In short: is the
oft-expressed complaint that managers have taken over the
universities to do with size, or are other factors at play?

There is absolutely no reason to assume that a university
should work differently from a business when it comes to
achieving efficiency advantages. Buildings, procurement,
facilities: scale affects all of these and there are economies of
scale to be gained. It should thus come as no surprise that serious attempts have been made to achieve such advantages,
certainly when financial resources are dwindling. From this
perspective, a number of trends are very understandable:
centralization of facilities and positions, and also partnerships or even mergers between institutions in order to

achieve economies of scale. But with all these measures, the degree of centralization is inevitably strengthened, and the distance between management and employees therefore becomes ever greater. This demands a constant search for the optimal balance between efficiency, centralization and size. A recent overview[1] has also shown that the larger an institution is, the more need there is to define decentralized units that are able to make their own decisions; otherwise, soon little is left of the autonomy of lecturers and students.

Another consequence of having larger and larger universities is that a wide gap emerges between administrators and the rank and file. Administrators feel obliged to deal optimally with the resources they have to manage, but often fail to explain this sufficiently well, and justify measures mainly in financial, not substantive, terms. What is more, the accumulation of measures often comes over not only as an invasion of freedom, but even more so, as lacking the trust to allow decentralized decision-making. In the Netherlands, 'output-driven thinking' in education has become symbolic of pernicious management, even though generally speaking it is about using limited funds to enable as many students as possible to study.

The growth of bureaucracy

All the same, it appears that much of the dissatisfaction is a result not only of efficiency measures, but perhaps even more of continuously having to account to government for the large sums that are invested from the public purse. Extensive justification is required for both teaching and

1   *Times Higher Education*, 2014: 'Super Size Me', November 2014.

research resources, in part because the government has to justify the decision to invest in education – rather than in other sectors, such as public health – on quality grounds. The prominent British professor of linguistics, Terry Eagleton, has described 'the death of the university'[2] largely as a consequence of the growth of bureaucracy, and many would agree with him. It is not for nothing that countries such as England and the US, and also Belgium and the Netherlands, have seen the emergence of a fierce debate about the ever-increasing pressure of regulation.

The sharp increase in bureaucracy – an increase that is not only claimed by cynical staff, but also backed up by the available statistics – puts a heavy burden on the future of the university. The figures alone show that the relationship between academic and non-academic personnel has shifted significantly in recent years in favour of the non-academic category, and that tensions between administrators and academics are increasing. The latter group reproaches the former for the fact that as checks and centralization increase, the focus has come to lie not on the academic, but on the administrator. According to academics, administrators are thereby disavowing their real role, namely of supporting and thus being subordinate to the academics who produce the teaching and research.[3] The Dutch social scientists Van Rinsum and De Ruijter[4] also identify this problem, and describe how

2   Eagleton, T., 2015: 'The Slow Death of the University', *The Chronicle of Higher Education*, April 6, 2015.

3   *Times Higher Education*, 2015: 'Keeping the Peace'. May 2015.

4   Van Rinsum, H. & A. de Ruijter, 2010: 'Van Primus inter pares in de Universitas tot chief executive officer in de McUniversity: de decaan als hybride functionaris'. In: Dorsman, L.J. & P.J. Knegtmans (eds), *Het universitaire bedrijf in Nederland, over professionalisering van onderzoek, onderwijs, bestuur en beheer*, 37-53, Verloren publishers.

much effort it takes to achieve effective working relations between the two groups. They draw particular attention to the key role that deans can play in this, and how they use a range of strategies for this purpose, to greater or lesser effect. Perhaps above all else, good leadership will also be essential in the future. The academic tribe demands primacy in this respect, and in my opinion rightly so; but in view of this, it is surprising to see how unwilling scholars have been to invest in such leadership. In essence, the accumulated problem of accountability and bureaucracy is a problem of trust, and more than size, lack of trust increasingly appears to be hampering universities: trust between the government and the institutions, between administrators and lecturers, between administrators and students. This problem will become more serious in the coming years if the university does not opt for different forms of organization and new forms of decision-making.

In addition to the effect on the quality of management, constant growth is having an effect on the quality of the institution itself.[5] In OECD countries, over 30% of the population on average participates in higher education, and this share is growing both within and beyond the OECD.[6] But it is inevitable that as participation rises, the quality of the students falls, as does the quality of the available staff. In the long term, the quality of the entire system of higher education will fall and, whilst the number of graduates will increase, the quality of the working population or of the knowledge economy will not necessarily increase as well.

5   Altbach, P.G., 2015: 'Massification and the Global Knowledge Economy: The Continuing Contradiction'. *International Higher education*. Special 20th Anniversary Feature: Higher Education's Future. Spring 2015.
6   OESO, 2014: *'Education at a Glance'*.

The problem is intensified when there is wide access to university education: whereas effective selection can limit the growing influx of students, in a low-threshold system, universities can grow explosively and will almost inevitably see a fall in quality. In this sense, the dilemmas connected to access and the ideal size of the university are closely related.

Whereas access to higher education in the US is under threat, as described above, it is interesting to compare this situation with that in the Netherlands, for example, where access, as in most Western European countries, is very broad. Access is granted simply by paying relatively low tuition fees and having finished adequate pre-university education. Problems relating to access are thereby avoided completely, and there is absolutely no risk of limiting access and ending up with a divided system as a result, as is the case in the US. A different problem is looming, however: universities are becoming too large, adequate-quality staff are either unavailable or unaffordable, and the quality of the students can leave much to be desired. The Netherlands thus serves as an example of a system in which, as a result of a lack of selection, students opt too readily for a research-intensive university when in many cases they would be better off at a college of higher vocational education. Part of the evidence for this claim lies in the relatively high drop-out rates in the first year, the large number of students who change programme, and the relatively low level of motivation that students have to study. The Dutch system is admittedly differentiated, and certainly more differentiated than in neighbouring countries, but hardly any use is made of this differentiation, because there is no system of referral based on selection. In such a system, there is increasing pressure on the universities and the size of the institutions is determined in practice by the market: more demand for places inevitably means growth, even to a size that is considered undesirable. Whereas countries such as the US and England use selection to refer less qualified students to more suitable forms of education, meaning that the size of universities can be managed *en passant* as a result, this is not possible in countries with a free admission system.

The optimal size for a university

In recent decades, other factors in addition to the growth in the student intake have also led to larger institutions, such as mergers. These are justified by arguments about economies of scale, but in a number of cases there is also a desire to achieve a wider range of courses or greater visibility, for example, to improve the university's chances in the rankings and funding. It is predicted that due to this last factor, the number of mergers will increase in the coming years, mainly between top institutions in the US and England.[7] Nevertheless, growth is often unpopular with both students and lecturers, due to strongly intensified feelings of anonymity and the unavoidable stretching of resources: when Manchester University merged with UMIST, the protests were so vehement that measures were hastily taken.

In fact, there is strikingly little research or formalized evidence available on the ideal size of a university: small enough not to be a massive business where everything is

7   *Times Higher Education*, 2015: 'More University Mergers on the Way, Predicts Legal Expert'. August 2015.

focused on production, but large enough to achieve economies of scale and, above all, to be sufficiently visible. In many informal debates, the size of the (private) top universities, which is often around 15,000 students or sometimes many fewer, is held up as an ideal. With such a size, advantages of scale are thought to be easily realizable. But the debates also suggest that beyond 20,000 students, the economies of scale appear to decrease and the disadvantages of more challenging management appear to multiply. And above all: the opinions of staff and students become more negative once one goes beyond this size, something that is also clear from student assessments, which in a number of countries are consistently in favour of smaller institutions. This underlines the fact that the university is not an ordinary business, and perhaps the difference is that the university flourishes best when the individual freedom of researchers is respected in relatively small communities.

This latter conclusion – that the university is not an ordinary business – suggests that where necessary, we should reform a culture that has gone too far in managing them as such. This certainly applies to Anglo-Saxon and Northern European countries, especially the Netherlands, where management based on commercial models appears to have penetrated the furthest. The university is in need of oxygen, whereas at present both teaching and research are suffocating in a flood of numerous business-like and bureaucratic processes. The onus here is primarily on the government: many of these processes have to do with the low-trust society in which we live, which has also infiltrated the universities. Auditing and having to account for every single detail are suffocating every possibility of developing one's own initiative.

There is also much to be done within the university, however. The classical structure of the university, which is to be found all over the world, needs to be held up to closer scrutiny. Many critical movements point to the fact that almost everything is focused on output and production: lots of publications, lots of teaching. Although important, this is not the greatest problem. After all, performance targets are also used elsewhere in society, and there is much within the university that exists by virtue of wanting to do things better than elsewhere – there is a highly competitive element to scholarship, which is valuable. Moreover, it is hard to make the case for why the university should be different, in this respect, from a hospital or a large firm. But the crux lies deeper; the crux is that scaling up and ever-expanding regulations create a climate of distrust and curtail professional autonomy. From administrators, this requires increasing reflection on ways to give back responsibility to researchers and lecturers, rather than regulating everything from the top down. From the 'shop floor', it demands leadership and discipline: performing more independently within the existing framework and taking full advantage of the opportunities. In this context, there should be greater rewards for entrepreneurship and creativity.

6.   The successes and failures of the entrepreneurial university

The notion of freedom of research – the ideal of completely independent scholarship – has existed since the Enlightenment. That scholarship should be independent is uncontroversial in many respects, but all too often this freedom is interpreted as meaning that the university, and the university alone, should be free to determine which research is important. The idea is particularly topical in relation to the extent to which the university should play an innovative role and make contributions that are relevant to society. In America, ever since Vannevar Bush's report there has been a relatively close relationship between universities and the private sector; but in Europe, too, universities are increasingly being paid by companies to conduct research. This is leading to friction and to criticism, especially within the universities, to the effect that the university risks putting its independence up for sale. Viewed from the opposite perspective, governments are demanding a say in the academic agenda in exchange for state funding, mainly in Asia, but also in Europe. This leads to the criticism that freedom of research is under threat. It is regarding this question of how to use this space between the universities, society and government where the most controversy is to be found.

There are major differences between the three continents in terms of how the universities function. This has much to do with the state of the economy, but also with culture. The street scene alone reveals major differences between the continents, differences that are also reflected in the university systems. In Northwestern Europe we see every sign of great prosperity, with excellent infrastructure and fine universities. Certainly, when compared with the US, England or Germany, it is clear that the Netherlands in particular and the Scandinavian countries spend lavish sums on university buildings. Although this continent is still wealthy, however, governments have less and less money to spend on education, partly due to the increasing costs of healthcare; and according to most scenarios, the economy is not set to grow so fast that the picture is likely to change in the future.

Asia, and particularly cities such as Hong Kong and Singapore, is enjoying rapidly growing prosperity and has an engaged, young population. Both cities have a dynamic, trendy atmosphere with fantastic infrastructure that is rapidly being developed and in many respects equals or even exceeds that in Europe. The universities enjoy less autonomy than European universities, and certainly than American ones, but they receive a lot of money from the government, which sets much store by knowledge, and the universities often have fantastic campuses. Economic growth will be considerable in the coming decades and the prospects for high levels of investment in education are good. Society is also globalizing in Asia: the media pays a relatively high degree of attention to the international situation, although the emphasis is still mainly on local politics, with what is evidently wary criticism and cautious treatment of the government.

With such images in mind, it is a shock to step into the metro in Boston: it is hard to imagine a more primitive or dirtier system. The trains appear to date from the pre-1960s, and also run as such. The roads in Boston are mediocre: the tunnels date from the last century and cause traffic jam after traffic jam. The universities do enjoy significant autonomy, but they sometimes reap bitter fruit from this: the government contribution continues to fall and public universities in particular are suffering as a result. The 'American century' appears to be drawing to a close, although this feeling is often concealed by nationalist slogans. Among the intellectual elite, though, the analysis is slowly penetrating that the US no longer dominates the world's stage. Many realize that the wars that the US lost or failed to win (Afghanistan, Iraq, Syria, Ukraine) are characteristic of a superpower in decline. It is telling that Joseph Nye recently published a book entitled 'Is the American Century Over?'[1]

The university as a motor of innovation

All of the above perhaps says more about the future than the past, however, for that is the light in which we should view the power and innovative strength of the American university system, with its showpieces such as Harvard and the Massachusetts Institute of Technology (MIT) – although there are striking differences between the two. Both institutions are among the best in the world, regardless of the ranking you consult. Both are private and have a high degree of autonomy. But this is where the similarities end. Harvard University is one of the oldest American institutions and entirely cast in the typical mould of the 'Great American Research University':[2] a foundational college system, in

[1]   Nye, J.S., 2015: *Is the American Century Over?*, Polity, 152 pp.
[2]   Crow and Dabars (2015) constantly refer to the 'Great' American Research University. This description is a good illustration of the fact that there is much complacency about the system in the US, but at the same time, the context reveals much concern about losing what is indeed a very powerful system.

which a considerable number of Bachelor's degrees are gained in the Liberal Arts College. This is followed by a graduate phase lasting five years, of which two years are course-based, corresponding with the Master's phase, followed by three years of doctoral research. Students rarely take self-standing Master's degrees; these are almost always seen as an intermediate stage on the way to the PhD. In this sense, it has become a binary system (Bachelor's phase followed by graduate school) with the Master's as the first part of the PhD, in contrast to the European system, which in accordance with the provisions of the 1999 Bologna Agreement has retained the characteristics of the three classical cycles.

Harvard (like MIT) is a small university by European standards, and like MIT it has around one thousand undergraduates a year who pay annual tuition fees of about $45,000. If one includes the campus fee for accommodation and food, this adds up to $60-65,000 per year, per student. Harvard is the incarnation of tradition, as is clearly evident on Commencement Day (the day on which degrees are awarded), and there is a reason for this: this tradition allows the university to maintain a large alumni network that forms the most important basis for financing; along with tuition fees, government contributions to research funding and contributions from private partners, gifts constitute the largest source of income. Amongst the twelve largest private universities, philanthropy is responsible for around 25% of income on average (figures for 2008-2009).[3] Harvard is in a different league from almost every other university, however: it had a programme that aimed to raise 6 billion

3   Lacroix, R. & L. Maheu, 2015: *Leading Research Universities in a Competitive World*, McGill-Queen's University Press.

dollars in donations for 2016, the anniversary year of both Harvard and Utrecht University in the Netherlands. Harvard had a total annual budget of 4.2 billion dollars in the 2013 financial year, and an endowment fund of 36.4 billion dollars in 2014. And all this for a university that, in terms of magnitude, is around two thirds the size of Utrecht University, for example: this makes its income around eight times larger than the annual budget of the average Dutch university, mainly through endowments (around 40%) and research grants, which always constitute at least 25% of the income. But this mix makes Harvard very sensitive to fluctuations, especially when it comes to the volume of gifts and investments. It was for this reason that the 2008 financial crisis resulted in dismissals for the first time in its history. Nevertheless, donations from the extremely loyal worldwide Harvard alumni network (323,000 living alumni, of whom 52,000 live in 201 countries other than the US) make it a formidable knowledge institution that will not be quick to let go of its current level of influence and impact. Its alumni are among the world's absolute *crème de la crème*, and Harvard will continue to form part of the backbone of America's knowledge economy.

MIT is organized differently: it is a technical university that is managed in a very decentralized way, where the departments enjoy a high degree of autonomy. The key to its success – perhaps even more so than at Harvard – lies in selecting the very best students and the very best professors. The motto is: select the top lecturers and researchers, pay them more-than-excellent salaries, and wait to see what happens. There is also a tendency, even more so than at Harvard, to hire faculty young and let them rise internally to senior positions, rather than bringing in top scientists at a later stage. The latter practice is not only extremely

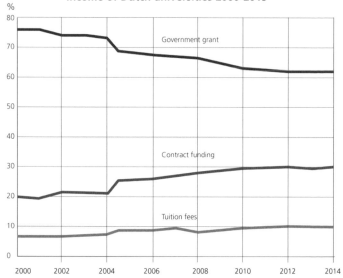

Income of Dutch universities 2000-2015

Government grant

Contract funding

Tuition fees

Fig. 6: Percentage shift in the incomes of Dutch universities between 2000 and 2014, mainly caused by the fall in the government's contribution and the increase in funding from third-party actors such as businesses and the EU. (Source: Rathenau)

expensive, but it also does not always produce the desired results within MIT's entrepreneurial culture. For it is an entrepreneurial institution: as is the case elsewhere in the US, after receiving a sum to start a lab (often around 1 million dollars), aside from their salary, academics are left entirely to their own devices. This principle is taken to extremes at MIT: a head of department who needs a new building (costing around 60-80 million dollars) only need knock on his dean's door once he has managed to raise half this sum. Subsequently, he and the dean stand a chance of getting a contribution of 25% of the building costs from the central administration, after which the faculty may pay the final 25%. The deans at MIT with whom I spoke

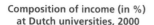

Composition of income (in %)
at Dutch universities, 2000

Composition of income (in %)
at Dutch universities, 2014

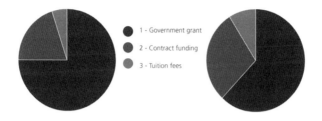

1 - Government grant

2 - Contract funding

3 - Tuition fees

Fig. 7: Development of the incomes of Dutch universities during the period between 2000 and 2014, as a percentage of the total lump sum, showing the falling state contribution and rising third-party funding and, to a lesser degree, rising tuition fees. (Source: Rathenau)

were therefore strikingly relaxed: there were no financial worries, at least, not for them.

One striking feature of MIT is the focus on interdisciplinary research. There are examples of pioneering convergences, interdisciplinary partnerships such as in cancer research, brain research and sustainability research, but also in the social sciences and the humanities. Every student at MIT has a thorough basis in science, technology, engineering and mathematics (STEM) – otherwise they would not have been admitted – but this does not stand in the way of pioneering non-technical or non-exact research (such as in history or drama!). Creative collaboration is the keyword, and everything at MIT is focused on connectedness: on linking people and fields with each other as accessibly as possible, in the hope that new, promising partnerships will emerge.

Harvard and MIT are not threatened by the crisis that is affecting the public universities, and each has its own great strengths. The secret lies in various factors, but in the end, what both institutions have in common is the huge pressure on faculty to generate funding. Competition is the most basic keyword here. The pressure is laid fair and square on the shoulders of the academics, however, who are of such a high quality that they usually succeed in getting the funding they want. But high quality or not, work stress is taken to a whole new level when one considers the number of research proposals that are written here, including by graduate students who want to attend conferences. First one writes the proposal, then one acquires funding via a competitive process; what's learned in the cradle lasts till the grave.

Besides the US, Asian universities are particularly entrepreneurial: they are enjoying growing success in valorization, and entrepreneurship is encouraged, even self-evident. Here, too, competition is fierce. The contrast with Europe is great, although in Europe the links with industry have also strengthened significantly in recent years, and entrepreneurship is being encouraged more and more. Figures 6 and 7 illustrate this picture. But European universities still count on a major contribution from the government for both teaching and research. Although this has some extremely positive aspects, as we saw in relation to access to the university, at the same time, universities complain about autonomy and automatically argue in response that the government should not demand anything in return for its investment, because this would encroach upon the freedom of research.

The 'freedom' of research

It is a fact that when pursuing external funding of whatever nature, universities run the risk of solving one problem only to end up with at least two new ones. In the first place, every financier demands a say in exchange for money, whether it is the state, a private company or a private benefactor. The problem is that this 'shift in say' can cut deeply into the functioning of the university. Many studies show that giving the state a voice usually leads to limits on autonomy, whereas it is precisely this autonomy that gives universities the power and flexibility to meet challenges: a study by the Association of European Universities has shown plain as day that the best performing universities have the most autonomy and the least state regulation.[4] But when giving the state a say is exchanged for giving other financiers a say, another danger looms, such as that expressed in the notion of valorization. This entails an exchange of knowledge, often for money and often with industrial partners, which inevitably results in research being steered in particular directions. In itself, this does not have to be a risk, so long as this applied research – for this is what industrial contracts often involve – does not take up too great a share and universities do not become dependent on it.

On paper, everyone agrees on the need for a balanced relationship between applied and curiosity-driven research, because it is very important to retain the capacity to explore new areas whilst at the same time solving current problems.[5] Aside from strategic considerations, however, maintaining a healthy relationship is not less important for the staff, lecturers and students, who need to be reassured that the freedom of research is not under threat. As it indeed often is: the need to acquire funding is already

4   Estermann, T., T. Terhi Nokkala & M. Steinel, 2011: 'University Autonomy in Europe II: The Scorecard'. EUA report.
5   Arnold, E. & F. Giarracca, 2012: Getting the Balance Right: Basic Research, Missions and Governance for Horizon 2020, Technopolis group, October 2012.

putting limits on this freedom, and these limits increase in step with the increasingly detailed conditions that are attached to financing, as is often the case for specific industrial contracts. This shows that it is essential to have a third form of financing to maintain the balance and to avoid a too great dependency on industry. One example is donations from private individuals, which is standard practice in Anglo-Saxon countries, and which can be large enough to counter these adverse tendencies.

The rise of valorization since the Second World War has created the impression that the university should not only be prepared to compensate falling state contributions with more money from the private sector, but that universities *should* contribute to the economy as a matter of course. In the US, there has always been a fairly strong relationship between the academic world and the industrial world, but in Europe this relationship is traditionally far less well-developed. Following the example set by Asia, in particular, where over the past few decades, successful technological innovation has had a significant impact on the European market, the European Union has initiated large-scale programmes to strengthen the connection between universities and industry. In the Netherlands in 2012, this even took the shape of a relationship between academic and industrial policy that resembled the approach taken by countries such as Singapore, which served as role models. Via the so-called top sectors, the universities were forced to contribute to particular areas where industry had a need. In order to promote this, the government gave preferential funding to these sectors, including funding that had previously been earmarked for free research. This immediately raises the question of whether universities should be used for such purposes. Is it the role of the university to contribute to the economy, and if so, to what degree? Shouldn't the government be ensuring that every university has sufficient funds for free and unrestricted research, rather than coercively steering research in particular directions, as happens in Singapore, for example?

In this sense, too, the dilemma of the freedom of research – which in fact relates to the autonomy of an institution – is more of a pressing problem than ever. Stefan Collini makes a rigorous case for freedom,[6] but in doing so he shifts the problem of financing unashamedly back onto the government's side of the table, arguing explicitly for a larger role on the part of government, especially when it comes to protecting the share of fundamental research. He omits to mention that in view of tight government budgets, government will simply not be in a position to pay for what has traditionally been a central responsibility. On the other hand, the universities have not yet truly explored the issue of what might constitute an effective middle-way between giving private funders a say and the falling financial power of government, and also between the university as an economic entity or as a bulwark of fundamental research.

But there is a third important element in this discussion, in addition to fundamental research and the economic contribution, and that is the societal contribution, which is not easy to express in financial terms. In Europe, in particular, this debate has accelerated since the EU put the Grand Societal Challenges at the heart of its science policy: more than ever before, major societal problems are being identified as the objective of research. In other words, this is not about economic contributions, but about what science brings to society, paired with increasingly loud calls for

6   Collini, S., 2012: *What Are Universities For?*, Penguin Books.

·essing this not in terms of valorization, but of impact. The former is mainly about the augmentation of value in the knowledge chain, whereas the latter alludes to the societal contribution that is made, even if no money has been earned with this in a direct sense.

All over the world, thus also in Europe, the humanities and social sciences are particularly critical of valorization. This undoubtedly has to do with the ability of these fields to earn money. After all, the natural sciences, medicine and the technological sciences find it easier than the arts or humanities to produce products or technologies. In turn, the latter rightly feel discriminated against if they are consequently seen as inferior or less productive disciplines and therefore receive much less funding. Certainly in the Netherlands, this feeling has been strengthened by the manner in which the top sector policy mixes industrial politics with scientific politics to an unprecedented degree.

It would give a significant boost to the debate about how research choices should be made if the value of scholarship were not measured largely in terms of economic yield, but were seen in the much broader terms of societal impact. For then one would suddenly get a completely different picture of the 'value' of scholarship, and with this, of the disciplines that should be encouraged by the government or the private sector. Think of solving the climate change problem, for example: in addition to a lot of technical expertise on climate change, a major contribution from the social sciences is also needed to change the behaviour – the enormous consumption of fossil fuels – that caused the problem in the first place. Or think of public health problems: in addition to medical knowledge, these largely require knowledge about how to influence behaviour in order to achieve prevention. Or think of the problem of immigration: in addition to technical issues relating to food production, for example, this problem requires new forms of governance and citizenship in a multicultural society. These are all matters for which having economically measurable contributions from scholars is not essential.

Scholarship is never 'free' in the sense that it is free from pressure from stakeholders and financers; this is a fiction that we should not hesitate to bury. Equally limited, however, is the simple idea that in addition to fundamental research, only innovation and the creation of economic value should be the objective of the university. The university is in need of new arrangements with the government and industry that clearly delineate where the university's freedom lies, but at the same time, clearly indicate where a legitimate call could be made on universities to solve the major problems that will affect society in future.

7. Under the spell of production and quality

The university has long played a major role in discovering knowledge without being subject to any clear quality criteria. Universities used to be supervised by a city, province or state, king or Pope, or whoever had set up the university. This supervision was often delegated to a board, which undertook the actual supervision on behalf of the founding person or institution. Today, though, universities across the world have entered new waters as a result of the culture of continuous public accountability for quality and production. This sometimes takes the form of strict state supervision of quality and financial accountability, but there is also increasing pressure from the rankings, which compare universities across the world based on what are often unclear criteria, and have a disruptive effect on the entire system.

For many centuries, establishing a university simply meant that the founding institution provided a sum of money that would cover the cost of the salaries and buildings. The key factor was reputation: a university was often known as very good (or bad) on the basis of a number of eminent professors, without there being much quantitative evidence for this. Reputation was established through the informal judgement of one's peers, although it was also important for scholars to keep an eye on their reputation among financiers. There are examples of scholars who, out of canny self-interest, took much trouble to get into the good books of a city's ruler or governors: this was a way to create opportunities for additional funding. The story of

Galileo Galilei, who had frequent problems with his salary and therefore sometimes had to make compromises, speaks volumes in this respect.[1]

Throughout the whole history of the university, until deep into the twentieth century, it was largely the quality of the teaching that determined an institution's reputation, whereby a professor's reputation was often established with a limited number of standard works. There was also absolutely no pressure to publish in the sense that numbers of publications were viewed as an indication of quality. The universities were small and clearly structured, and it would be fair to claim that the pressure of work was low compared with that in modern institutions. No one counted how much had been produced each year, although it was naturally the case that a person's reputation ultimately stood or fell on those few standard works that were published and that, of course, often contained a huge amount of work. And naturally, there were also bad universities that had extremely dubious reputations. One example is that of the University of Harderwijk, founded by the States of Gelderland in 1648 as the fourth university in the Netherlands, more as an object of prestige than because there was any great need for it. This university quickly acquired a questionable reputation, to the extent that popular rhymes even made allusions to how easy it was to obtain one's doctorate in Harderwijk. It is thus no wonder that its doors closed for good in 1811.

Universities operated in a relatively autonomous and isolated fashion until deep into the twentieth century. On the eve of the Second World War, the image of the ivory tower was still at its height, although the first changes to the system were already emerging. These became visible

1   Cohen, F., 2007: *De herschepping van de wereld*. Bert Bakker.

partly due to the growing tendency, from the beginning of the twentieth century, to publish separate articles rather than standard works, initially in the natural sciences, mathematics and medicine. This was stimulated in part by the ongoing intensification of the exchange of knowledge within a growing international community of scientists, whereby almost imperceptibly, peer review became the standard for monitoring the quality of the content.

The curse of metrics and rankings

It was only after the Second World War, however, and particularly with the growth of the universities as a result of the huge influx of students from the 1960s, that scholarly production increased formidably and simultaneously became highly internationalized. Given the academic supremacy of Anglo-Saxon countries at that time, English coincidentally became the academic lingua franca. Even in those early years of great growth, though, the universities mainly ran on reputations established among colleagues, whilst the pressure to publish, although admittedly greater than it had been at the beginning of the twentieth century, was still low in comparison with today's norm.

The great change occurred at the same time as the limits of growth were reached, whereby the huge expansion of the university system from the end of the 1980s led to problems in every Western country. Not coincidentally, around this time many governments made increasing use of professional quality assurance, initially in an attempt to keep a grip on the 'proper' investment of increasingly scarce funds. Private institutions were exempt from this, of course, but in the Netherlands, for instance, the government introduced

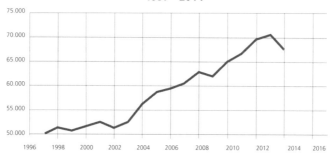

Total academic publications at Dutch universities, 1997 - 2014

Fig. 8: Increase in the number of scholarly publications in the Netherlands during the period between 1997 and 2014, showing exponential growth. (Source: Rathenau)

legislation whereby non-public, partly privatized universities were also able to receive government funding, but thereby became subject to the same quality assurance system as the public institutions. For the first time, quality was being measured systematically.

In the Netherlands, the establishment of this system of objectifying quality, something that was often equated with counting numbers of publications, led to an almost inconceivable increase in scholarly production. The number of publications per employee rose continuously, by a further 25% between 2000 and 2010,[2] making the Dutch system one of the most productive in the world, along with those of England and Switzerland, for example. This is shown in Figures 8 and 9. At first glance, there is nothing wrong with this; after all, society has a right to see public resources being invested effectively. An important factor lies behind this, however: with the introduction of the system, the measure

2   VSNU, 2012: 'Prestaties in perspectief. Trendrapportage universiteiten 2000-2020'.

Academic production per 100 FTE

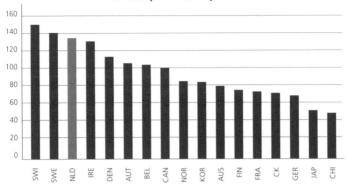

Fig. 9: Comparison of the scholarly production in 2015 in seventeen OECD countries, normalized per 100 FTE in order to achieve comparable data. The extremely high level of production in the Netherlands and other Northern European countries is striking. (Source: Rathenau)

of quality changed. No longer was qualitative assessment by one's peers the measure of things, but instead, the number of publications gradually became the key norm for quality and good performance. At every level, the university became the plaything of metrics, whereby university boards and external parties set conditions that steered scholarship more in the direction of production and away from content.

It is easy, but not entirely incorrect, to see this trend towards measuring quality by measuring production as part of a broader movement that emerged in the 1980s. In industry and in government, setting targets by using so-called key performance indicators also became the dominant model, one that arose in the Anglo-Saxon world and spread quickly. This was more than just an administrative model, or a management vision for keeping everything under control. Following the policies of Ronald Reagan in the US and Margaret Thatcher in the United Kingdom, which had been inspired by the theories of economists such as Milton Friedman, a neoliberal vision came to the fore across the world in which the individual, and thereby individual performance, became more and more important. Whereas this had been the case much earlier in the US, where it was rooted in a strong liberal tradition, through politicians such as Margaret Thatcher this view quickly gained ground in England and Europe at the end of the 1980s. The performance of the group or the reputation of the university was pushed into the background, to be replaced by the performance and the reputation of the individual. The gradual reaching of the limits of university growth, whereby governments had to demand greater accountability for the resources they invested, thereby went hand in hand with a new approach to measuring performance. Although it was not fully realized at the time, around thirty years ago, a spiral was set in motion of increased measurement and increased steering with respect to output.

In the course of this development, it is easy to understand how rankings quickly became more important for universities. Although the first rankings were only produced just over ten years ago, there is now a large number, all based on qualities that tend to be easy to measure: number of published articles, the type of journals in which articles are published, Nobel prizes and numbers of international students, as well as more subjective issues such as reputation. But all of the rankings pay more attention to research than teaching. This is not only because this has been the distinguishing feature of the university since Von Humboldt's time, but also because it is easier to measure – for example, via the number of publications – than the quality of teaching. Teaching is at risk of suffering as a result, because it is not, or is hardly, the focus of 'ranking management'. This confirms the impression that after eight hundred years, the university has definitively evolved from being a teaching institution where research takes place, into a research institution that provides teaching.

In this game of 'the numbers say it all', in the 1980s, major publishing companies developed an interest in the commercial publishing of scholarly articles, the 'impact' of which was reported with greater and greater emphasis. The market had grown large in the meantime and was also constantly expanding, and the demand for quality and for measuring quality had increased and was constantly increasing. There was room for a high level of differentiation in order to accommodate the growing influx of articles, in the form of increasingly specialized journals with an increasingly wide spread of reputations. Deliberately and systematically, this market was developed, expanded and made more differentiated by very large publishing firms such as Elsevier, with increasing attention paid to impact and the measurement of citations, capitalizing on the demand for these data in the assessment and rankings game.

Given this whole spiral of developments, after a relatively short period of time we find ourselves in a situation where governments are paying more and more attention to rankings to determine whether they are spending their money well, rankings are increasingly dependent on output, that output is increasingly measured in terms of impact and quality, and the freedom and pressure of work at universities is thereby increasingly being encroached upon. 'Publish or perish' is becoming an ever more apt description of the culture in which individual scholars find themselves, certainly during the period in which they have to get a permanent job, because such jobs are awarded largely on the basis of a publication record.

In the course of recent decades, the development of this spiral of publishing and rankings has insidiously had another effect: universities have become more dependent upon large publishing companies and major journals. How much one publishes and where have become so important that the university has, to a certain extent, sold its soul to the devil: at any rate, failing to publish enough in top journals causes a university to fall in the rankings, making it less attractive to students and thus costs money! But the foundations of the system are also financially unsustainable: if one succeeds in getting published in a top journal with research that is often financed by public means, a very considerable sum has to be paid in order to read that article. First, the major journals and publishers created an important market, then they had third-party-funded research delivered for free, and then they demanded a fee for this in the form of ever-rising subscription fees for an ever-growing number of journals. For the first time in forty years, this 'double dipping' is now leading to political and academic protest, especially in the US and Europe, and pressure to enable open access will undoubtedly grow further in the near future.

A recent report makes it clear that on the one hand, metrics – the use of key figures – appears unavoidable: 'Within the culture shifts, metrics are positioned as tools that can drive organizational financial performance as a key part of an institution's competitiveness'. On the other hand, the report clearly points to the risks this brings for integrity, because 'researchers cut corners or even cheat outright', and even because 'vice chancellors have huge chunks of their pay packet pegged to the performance in a league table'.[3] The report does not state how the spiral of metrics and rankings might be broken.

3   Wilsdon, J., et al., 2015: *The Metric Tide: Report of the Independent Review of the Role of Metrics in Research Assessment and Management.* DOI: 10.13140/

Reaching the limits

This whole complex – monitoring quality by measuring output, meaning that the importance of scholarly production in the form of publications increases; the resulting explosion in the number of publications that are produced each year and that, due to the deluge, are read less and less in relative terms; the resulting expansion in the academic publishing market, accompanied by the ever-higher pricing of this same output via astronomically rising subscription fees with a global value of 10 billion euros in 2011; with which the circle is closed, because it is on this output that the rankings system largely rests, on the basis of which governments invest – this whole complex now threatens to run aground.

In recent years, it has become increasingly clear that in addition to the rise of mass education and all of its consequences, this is where the modern university's second core problem lies: the design of the research process, its funding, the way in which attempts to control quality are increasingly shifting towards measuring production and rankings, in which teaching no longer counts at all. But also because the incentives across the whole system are increasingly focused on publishing more, whereby the peer-review system, once so lauded, is increasingly failing, often due to the torrent of publications. Not only that, but it has become increasingly clear that the emphasis on publishing large amounts has created perverse incentives that can facilitate fraud, for example.

As a result of all these problems, the whole system in which academia is imprisoned has been the subject of

RG.2.1.4929.1363. HEFCE. See also: *Times Higher Education*, 2015: 'The Weight of Numbers'. July 2015.

growing criticism since 2010. Through publications by Science in Transition[4] and, for example, the San Francisco Declaration,[5] since 2012, there have been pleas for the system to be thoroughly reformed. The first group is mainly concerned with the deluge of publications, some of which are of moderate added value, in a system in which all the incentives are focused on production. Although the biomedical sector is the ultimate symbol of this, the picture is recognizable more broadly. At the same time, these critics have supporters on the side of the university who point to the negative effects of the system on teaching, particularly through the constant encouragement of research, for this is mainly how reputations are established.[6]

This and other movements rapidly added their voices to growing discontent with the publishing industry, whereby criticism of 'double dipping' and the costs of the system led in 2015 to an all-out confrontation between the universities and the publishers. The governments in England and the Netherlands, for example, as well as the European Commission, had already taken clear positions on open access – that is to say, making all results of research, which is often funded from public means, publicly available. Universities in the Netherlands, in 2015, followed by those from England, Germany and Finland in 2016, refused to pay the traditional fee for publishers. They argued for lower fees and demanded open access. And in an extension to

4   Dijstelbloem, H., F. Huisman, F. Miedema & W. Mijnhardt, 2013: 'Waarom de wetenschap niet werkt zoals het moet, en wat daaraan te doen is'. *Science in Transition*, Position paper 2013. For a critical discussion of the peer review system, see also *Times Higher Education*, 2015: 'Peering into the Past'. June 2015.

5   San Francisco Declaration, 2013: http://www.ascb.org/dora/.

6   Verbrugge, A., J. van Baardwijk, (eds), 2014: *Waartoe is de universiteit op aarde?*, Boom.

this, the debate around open science is now in full swing, culminating in the Amsterdam Call for Action on Open Science.[7] This forms a final step for now in the process whereby the university has definitively left its ivory tower, while simultaneously reconsidering its core values, the question of the relationship between teaching and research, and, most profoundly of all, the question of who universities are there for in the first place. The Amsterdam Call raises themes such as change in the way in which quality is assessed, how to reward performance in a way that is less focused on research alone, how to make scholarly data and knowledge publicly available, and more involvement of societal stakeholders in setting up programmes and the use of scientific results.

All of these movements make it clear that the university should now start to reflect actively, at all levels, on how to manage its definitive departure from the ivory tower. With this, the nostalgia for the past, a simple return to *Bildung*, which is supported by some protest movements, will be impossible to realize. The universities will have to take steps forwards, not backwards, and will have to learn to profit from the entirely new approach to scholarship that is on the horizon: digital, in rapidly alternating coalitions or convergences, with a new manner of assessing and evaluating transparent and public scholarship, almost comparable to the way in which Wikipedia emerged. Knowledge will increasingly be shaped in the public domain, in increasingly informal relations. This has its disadvantages, but also offers a huge opportunity to break through the spiral of output and rankings described above.

7   Amsterdam Call for Action on Open Science, 2016: https://www.eu2016.nl/ documenten/rapporten/2016/04/04/amsterdam-call-for-action-on-open-science.

To break free of the current straitjacket of control, protocol and key performance indicators, Helga Nowotny argues that much more uncertainty and latitude should be allowed for scientific freedom and surprise results.[8] This is an argument that is really worth considering, because it gets to the heart of scholarship, namely, the conquering of unknown territory. This makes scholarship a pre-eminently uncertain process in terms of outcomes, meaning that focusing strictly on outcomes undermines the process. But this requires us to reform numerous processes, and it means that the university needs to be restructured completely: not only by providing different incentives, but by looking completely differently at what and who should steer the process of teaching and research. This unequivocally means that there should be more autonomy for individual lecturers and researchers, because it is there in particular that freedom and uncertainty play a role in achieving academic progress.

At the same time, Ronald Barnett[9] rightly pleads for the creation of a joint vision on the university of the future, beyond what he calls the entrepreneurial or developmental university and towards a much more flexible university that forms part of society and moves in a much more dynamic context. Barnett's 'liquid university' could be an intermediary phase on the way to the university of the future.

---

8   Nowotny, H., 2015: *The Cunning of Uncertainty*, Polity. A broad and penetrating examination of the fundamental principles of science. Critics point to the role that Nowotny played as president of the ERC, where prestigious grants were awarded mainly on the basis of metrics. Nowotny's book is a plea for more of a 'trial and error' approach in science, but critics also point to the need for 'planning and prediction' (see the pointed review by Stilgoe in 'Issues' in *Science and Technology*, 2016).

9   Barnett, R., 2011: *Being a University*, Routledge, 188 pp.

Part 2
The key factors in the coming decades

In this part, we explore the surroundings in which universities will be operating in the coming 25 years. What are the key factors that are going to influence and change the system? Some are easy to identify. Information technology will certainly continue to influence higher education, but precisely how it will do so is not easy to predict: are we still at the beginning of a revolution, or will change be gradual from now onwards? Scholarship will undoubtedly become more dynamic as a result of IT and will be conducted in interdisciplinary research combinations that are subject to increasingly rapid change. Knowledge will be omnipresent and available everywhere, but the effective use of knowledge will increasingly be complicated by an overwhelming flow of data. Other trends are also emerging. Continuing urbanization is leading to mega-cities that, as the global knowledge hubs of the future, will likely play a determining role in the most visible developments in science, particularly in technological fields. Fundamental changes in the labour market are making themselves felt, but they also raise many questions. One thing that is certain is that the economic outlook and the degree of prosperity have always played a determining role in the development of education, and this will remain the case. This means that with the changing economic balance of power, the global relationship between knowledge-powers will change radically. Asia is gaining ground: the war for talent is on!

8.   The key trends

The hustle and bustle of everyday life leaves little time for reflection – even in universities, where one would expect reflection to be one of the main activities. There is also little space to reflect on the future, and even when we do, we tend to think in terms of the situation today and much less in terms of that of tomorrow. Nevertheless, the changes that are occurring in the world are more radical and more rapid than ever before. This compels us to reflect on the changed circumstances in which the university of the future will have to operate, even if these statements have uncomfortable implications. For these predictions are surrounded by great uncertainty. The opposite is also true, however: we can be certain that the university that does not dare to make predictions will not survive.

Given that it is difficult to make accurate predictions a year in advance and that it is almost impossible to look further than five years ahead, wanting to make predictions for 2040 seems ridiculous. Social dynamics are so great that the world changes from week to week and from month to month. The economy fluctuates massively, the financial markets are volatile, and relations between states are constantly changing. In short, making predictions is of limited value; in the context of the university, Nowotny even sees this as a major element of governance that leads to a disastrous straitjacket of false security.[1] At the same time, it is undoubtedly the case that there is a beneficial aspect to predicting where scholarship is headed, because

---

1   Nowotny, H., 2015: *The Cunning of Uncertainty*, Polity, 198 pp.

research has long shown the important effect of the self-fulfilling prophecy.[2]

From a financial perspective, too, it is not irrational to want to know what the world might be like in 25 years' time, because every university takes investment decisions that anticipate such long periods. To take the example of real estate alone: at forty to fifty years, the average lifespan of a university building is almost double this. Moreover, most universities have already planned significant investments for the coming ten years at least: in the Netherlands in 2016, this involved a total investment of at least 3 billion euros.[3] But what would happen to all these investments if there were a large-scale shift to digital teaching?

As a thought experiment, we could look back 25 years to see what has changed and whether we could learn something from this when looking ahead to 2040. Admittedly, the world in 1990 looked completely different from how it does today, but the contours of our present society were starting to become clear. One could see, for example, that a reordering of political relations between East and West was occurring, although only the very beginning of the far-reaching thaw between the two power blocks was evident at that time. Something that would have been completely implausible in 1990, however, did nevertheless occur in the period between 2012 and 2015: after the thaw, there was another drastic deterioration in relations between East and West. It was unpredictable, in other words.

In 1990, it was already becoming clear that countries such as China had the potential to become powerful economies,

2   Martin, B.R. & R. Johnston, 1999: 'Technology Foresight for Wiring Up the National Innovation System: Experiences in Britain, Australia, and New Zealand', *Technological Forecasting and Social Change* 60(1): 37-54.
3   Onderwijsinspectie, 2016: *'Rapport huisvesting MBO, HBO, en WO'*.

but no one foresaw that this would happen so fast, or that economic relations – and with them, political power relations – would change so fundamentally that traditional economic great powers, such as the US and Europe, would be overtaken in the meantime. Although the situation in the Middle East was already troubled in the 1990s, it appeared that this would involve regional conflicts that would give rise to concern, but would remain limited. Ever since the Arab Spring of 2012, however, the Middle East has been in flames, the region is the site of the largest conflict since the Second World War, and there has been an unprecedented flow of migrants from this region and North Africa that will lead to radical changes in North-South relations.

Economic growth and decline have proved equally unpredictable. Although there were admittedly signs of growth in the global economy in 1990, back then, no one dared dream of almost two decades of unprecedented prosperity, which was of course also shaped by the opening up of markets in Asia and South America. But no one, even in the most pessimistic scenarios, predicted the collapse of the financial markets and the banking system in 2008, which led to the worst economic crisis the world had seen since the 1920s.

Looking back, however, other developments also seem astonishing. The 1980s saw the introduction and relatively rapid expansion of the use of the PC or personal computer, so called because until then only mainframes or larger computers had been used by multiple users at the same time. In 1990, no one was able to foresee that the growth and technological development of PCs would be so explosive. And not only that; whole aspects of society have become dependent on computer-controlled technology, including the street lighting. The impact that digital technology has is staggering, not only in relation to controlling social processes, but even in relation to shaping them. Take the internet, for example, or Wikipedia: hardly imaginable developments that have taken place largely over the last 25 years.

We could say the same of communications: whilst the mobile phone was not new 25 years ago, back then, it would have been hard to foresee its technological development in combination with its global distribution. Eighteen million mobile telephones with connections are sold every year in India alone.[4] In combination with the rapidly expanding telephone system and the introduction of the smart phone, a boom in social media has taken place in recent years: gathering and providing information and consulting visual material are having an unprecedented impact on social life. The amount of data that is available on the Internet, and the amount of data that we can process using computers that are relatively cheap and easy to access, are leading to a new and unforeseen form of science. The exploration of big data is a surprisingly productive field, in which the analysis of patterns in unimaginably large quantities of data is giving rise to completely new insights.

None of this could be predicted back in 1990, let alone 25 years before that. In 1990, however, many trends were already visible and some relatively good predictions were made; sometimes, certain patterns can even be traced back to 1965, and predications from that era have in some cases stood the test of time around fifty years later. One such example is the growth in the global population, which has grown as predicted, based on scenarios from the 1970s. Although the estimates have been adjusted upwards, it

4   Ericson, 2014: 'Q4 report, 2014'.

would seem reasonable to extrapolate this growth into the future using improved models. Related to the growth in the global population, in the past fifty years there has been an unprecedented shift from rural areas to the cities. Whereas the predictions on population growth that were made in the 1970s were relatively accurate, as shown by the example of the report of the Club of Rome, it would only become clear in the 1980s that the migration to the cities that was underway would continue, and that in Asia this would soon lead to the development of extremely large cities. And it was only at the beginning of this century that we realized that this constant migration to the city could lead to super-cities; and since 2010, the growth has been so rapid that mega-cities will emerge in the near future, which will bring an entirely new dynamic over the coming 25 years.

Twenty-five years ago, scenarios with reasonable predictive power on the intensification of transport were already being outlined. Looking at patterns in transportation in the US, it had already become clear at that time that there would be rapid expansion in the aviation industry. The same was true of road and rail transport, although no one was able to foresee that a country like China would be able to build a network of high-speed trains at such an astonishingly high speed. The image of the global village, which stems from the 1990s, is being realized to the full.

The outcomes of predictions on the availability of energy and raw materials have also turned out better than feared. Although the reports of the Club of Rome have been roundly criticized, and it has to be acknowledged that the detailed predictions indeed proved incorrect, the reports did serve as a timely warning signal for rapidly dwindling energy supplies. The same is true of the availability of many other raw materials, including water and forests. The predictions left much to be desired in a quantitative sense, of course, but the predicted scarcity of raw materials and even food is in fact increasingly materializing, despite all the technological ingenuity that has been dedicated to reversing this scarcity in the intervening decades. In other words, this was predictable.

Looking to the future in the context of higher education, four phenomena stand out. All are related to deep underlying changes in the social order, whereby we can expect them to continue in one form or another, and to have an impact on the future of the university. First of all, the potential development of the great economic blocks: there has already been much speculation to this effect in the scenarios developed, among others, by governments like the Dutch one,[5] the EU,[6] and the World Economic Forum in Davos.[7] Although the extent to which and speed with which these developments will take place remains unclear, a fundamental shift in the economic balance of power seems inevitable. A second change concerns far-reaching urbanization, which will certainly play a significant role in the development of the world's future knowledge centres. Third, it is already clear that IT and all forms of digitization of communication and knowledge will have a large impact on the social order and, by extension, the universities. Together, these three phenomena will, to a large degree, determine a fourth factor, namely the development of the

5   Ministerie van Onderwijs, Wetenschappen en Cultuur, 2015: *Nederland 2035: trends en uitdagingen.*
6   VERA, 2015: *Policy Brief: Evolving Dimensions of the European research and Innovation Landscape.*
7   Carey, K., 2015: 'Are We about to See the End of Universities as We Know Them?', *World Economic Forum*, April 29, 2015. See also: *World Economic Forum*, 2015: 'Global Strategic Foresight Community – Member's Perspective on Global Shifts'.

labour market versus the educational level of the global population.

Since the 2008 financial crisis, another trend has emerged, the implications of which are still very unclear. Since this time, when the fragility of the global financial system became apparent, a steady shift has been taking place worldwide towards an increasingly nationalist political climate with a growing focus on regional interests, inevitably resulting in building tensions between individual countries. The era of globalisation and ongoing expansion of trade and transport, with ever-increasing flows of people to even the most closed of countries, appears to be over. In the past few decades this resulted in an unprecedented flourishing of science in terms of scientific exchange, as well as the rise of science in, for example, Asia and South America. The exchange of students and knowledge reached its apex around the turn of the century, with the establishment of many foreign campuses in Asia by universities predominantly based in the English-speaking world.

It seems, however, that this situation has come to an end, at least for now. On all fronts, people are reacting against the dominant neoliberal paradigm of free trade and free exchange of knowledge. Looking back, this increasing globalisation was driven mainly by the markets, and the Western economies – the US and the UK in particular, but Europe too – significantly benefited from the influx of talent from Asia into Western countries and the contribution these people were able to make to economic growth and innovation. But it is clear that the tide has turned. The Chinese Minister of Education already stated back in 2015 that too much intervention in education by other countries was considered undesirable. The 2014 student protests in Hong Kong are a clear sign of the times, as the

Chinese government is increasingly curtailing freedom. Since 2010, Russia has pursued a strongly nationalist agenda which attempts to formulate a response to the expansion of Western influence in the former Eastern Bloc countries. But the events in Europe and the US show that here, too, nationalist sentiment is on the rise, as illustrated by Brexit and the election of Donald Trump in the US.

Since the Arab Spring, this polarisation has acquired a new dimension with the rise of Islamic fundamentalism, which finds its breeding ground in the great public dissatisfaction with the economic situation in countries which, in the past few decades, have largely been ruled by dictators and whose populations have not benefited from the growth in prosperity. This prosperity was often shipped away from these countries in the form of raw materials. The world is entering into a new era defined by sharp contrasts and increasing protectionism. This is bound to have a major impact on the academic world, and the extent to which knowledge and talent can be exchanged internationally.

These developments appear so robust, and the impact on the future of the university so clear, that we should undoubtedly address them here. But what to think of all those other issues: climate change, the scarcity of raw materials, food and water, and the weakening of institutions? Or problems relating to economic migration and the refugee crisis resulting from wars, which have deep roots in the decline of governmental power, climate change and the availability of raw materials? Although they are more difficult to predict, these changes are so fundamental that the university will also inevitably be affected by them. It is clear that the social role that the university wishes to play, and indeed must play, will thereby change: in view of the magnitude of the problems, the university will have to get involved in finding solutions, whether it wants to or not. If it does not, its societal foundations and even its legitimacy will be brought into question.

9.   The economy determines the future

Almost all analyses agree that the coming years will see a far-reaching shift in the global economic balance of power. Whereas in past decades the US and Europe were the most powerful economies, it is clear that Asia, led by China, will outstrip the two old power blocks. It is also clear that South America, and perhaps also Africa, will play a meaningful role on the global economic stage. Throughout their long history, universities have been deeply dependent upon the level of prosperity. A rise would often mean that the university expanded, whereas economic decline would result in contraction, particularly in higher education. The global knowledge landscape will thus change radically in the coming decades as a result of these shifts.

The relationship between prosperity and rising demand for higher education is not a simple one. On the one hand, it is often the result of targeted government policies that see a well-educated professional population as essential for economic growth. On the other hand, there is a strong societal effect: parents encourage their children to get a university education so that they can have what they themselves never had, namely a good job and a high income. In today's rapidly growing Asian economies in particular, for example, upward social mobility over the generations is still possible, whereas it has become much more difficult in the US and Europe. Given the high level of education among Western populations, there will have to be an acceptance that downward social mobility will be more common than in the past, with all the problems this brings. Moreover, this also implies a revaluation of the professions, whereby graduates will not necessarily get the best-paid jobs, simply because there will be a large supply of graduates and scarcity in other occupational groups.

The global rise in demand for higher education requires enormous investment. China and India are facing the mammoth task of expanding the number of universities and colleges of professional education in their countries by what may be a factor of 100[1] in order to be able to meet this demand. However, these countries – especially China and other increasingly affluent countries – are able to do this due to their level of economic growth, which is set to continue in the coming years. By comparison, the level of economic growth in Europe is likely to be much lower: predictions suggest that in the coming years, we should not count on having the same level of growth that we saw in the first years of this millennium, let alone growth such as that in Asia. In both the US and Europe, the combination of relatively limited economic growth plus the significant ageing of the population will perpetuate the trend towards governments that have to make tricky choices and that need increasing sums of money for public health, and thus have less and less money available for education. In the coming years in Asia, by contrast, there will be far-reaching investment in the expansion of education, which means that expanding university education will also be high on the agenda. Global power relations between the universities will change fundamentally as a result: if, until now, Western universities have automatically played a leading role, in future, this will no longer be the case. Economic growth in Asian countries, in particular, will rapidly lead to these university systems enjoying greater power.

1   *International Higher Education*, 2015: 'Special 20th Anniversary Feature: Higher Education's Future'. Spring 2015.

In countries where government is on the retreat, this will initially take the form of less investment in tertiary education: the notion that both primary and secondary education are among a government's core tasks is such a deeply-rooted conviction around the world that this is not likely to change any time soon. In the US and England, history has shown that the government can indeed withdraw from the university education sector easily and quickly. This is always legitimized with reference to the profit principle: tuition fees are simply increased with reference to the argument that students with a university education will be able to find better jobs, which will make it possible to earn back the rising cost of education. But university education is thereby no longer seen as something that is in the interests of the nation, but something that is more in the interests of the individual, who purchases a good future for himself and has to pay for it himself. Steps have also been taken down this path in the Netherlands, and it will be difficult to turn back: what were until now general student grants will shortly be abolished altogether. They will be replaced by what is admittedly an excellent loans system, but this cannot be interpreted as anything other than a clear indication of a retreating government.

This privatization will undoubtedly lead to falling participation in higher education: the US's sharp fall in the OECD rankings of higher education graduates as part of the total labour force is revealing in this respect.[2] When it comes to illustrating the gravity of government withdrawal on economic or political grounds, it is sufficient to quote Sexton:[3]

2   OESO, 2011: 'Education at a glance'.
3   Sexton, J., 2014: Access that Matters: Quality Education for All. Unpublished address, November 2, 2014.

I worry about American higher education, not only as the president of a university but also as a citizen. I worry that too many people – from pundits to politicians to philanthropists – are pressing policies that sound attractive but will do great harm to the quality of what our colleges and universities do and to the equality of meaningful access for talented citizens born in the wrong zip code. I worry that higher education, long the instrument of upward mobility, will become the tool of social stratification. I worry that leaders who avidly seek seats for their own children in the nation's best (and often most expensive) schools, colleges and universities (from $30,000 kindergartens to $60,000 colleges) will rest easily having unintentionally relegated the children of the poor, the middle class, the uninformed, and the unconnected to colleges or universities to which they would never send their own progeny.

If we add to this that education is increasingly becoming a characteristic of social class,[3] it is clear that a dichotomy in the higher education system will leave deep scars in society.

The sense of a growing divide, not only in the US but also in Europe, is supported by statistics. There exists an educated elite which benefits from the increasing prosperity, but a growing proportion of the population is faced with a decline in opportunities on the labour market and does not have access to the quality education that is essential to compete in this increasingly-international market. The negative sentiment of the 'angry white man' who is losing out, or feels he is losing out, to globalisation and the open borders that promote international trade, has grown over the past few years. This resulted in the disaffection that coloured the elections in the US, brought about the shift in the British electorate, and dominated polls, referendums and elections in the Netherlands, Italy, France and Germany. Here an increasing rift has become, and will continue to be, apparent between an elite which benefits from the effects of globalisation and sets the national political agenda, and which predominantly lives in the major cities, and the populations in the rural or industrial areas who feel increasingly as if they are not heard and cannot actively take part in the political process.

The universities are undeniably on the side of the elite.[4] This is evident not only from the fact that the job market for graduates remains relatively favourable, but sometimes also literally from the way the institutions present themselves as 'elite' universities and 'Ivy League'. This is underlined by the high tuition fees which, despite the extensive possibilities for financial aid that exist, often remain beyond the reach of ordinary citizens. In 2014, a rather extensive study was conducted in the Netherlands that looked into the causes and consequences of the gap that exists between these two worlds.[5] This research also demonstrated that an individual's level of education is very important: it turns out that this is increasingly the factor that determines their role and position in society. The conclusion of this study is that the higher someone's level of education, the higher the cultural capital they have at their disposal. As a result, they demonstrate less negativity toward groups in society with different repertoires of thought, feeling and behaviour. The higher educated have more social skills, social insight, and, above all, political confidence. This suggests that the differences between the two groups partly stem from

4   Hawking, S., 2016: 'This Is the Most Dangerous Time for Our Planet'. *The Guardian*, 1 December.
5   Bovens, M., P. Dekker & W. Tiemeijer, 2014: *Gescheiden werelden? Een verkenning van sociaal-culturele tegenstellingen in Nederland*. Sociaal Cultureel Planbureau en WRR.

the disparity in feelings of social vulnerability, cultural insecurity and political powerlessness. This outcome only constitutes further evidence for the conclusion that universities are almost, by definition, on the side of the elite.

The elite position of the academic world will increasingly meet with criticism. To start with, criticism such as in the US, where Trump is all too aware that globalisation is not in the interests of the 'angry white man', whereas universities clearly stand to benefit from it. In addition, populist parties in the US and Europe express pointed criticism of universities for being expensive and bureaucratic. But what is much more fundamental is the growing and deep distrust of an intellectual elite which feels that facts and common sense are on its side. This disregards, however, the reality that facts barely play a role and that the debate is primarily governed by emotion. This is also evident from people's reactions on social media, where facts are no longer recognised as facts, and are instead dismissed as mere opinions. Here, too, Trump has set a new record: his statement that 'a lot of people feel it wasn't a proper certificate' after President Obama had published his birth certificate is emblematic of the 'post-fact' era that we are entering into.[6]

The shifting economic balance will leave a further scar in the global university landscape in the coming 25 years. This relates to the maxim that talent always searches for optimal funding, and will therefore move to new centres of wealth. The war for talent can already be felt, owing to the fact that the flow of talented scientists is increasingly directed not towards the US, but towards Asia. Also Europe,

6   For some context see also Fukuyama, F., 2017: 'The Emergence of a Post-Fact World'. *NewEurope*, January 8, 2017; Stiglitz, J.E., 2017: 'The Age of Trump'. *NewEurope*, January 8, 2017.

through programmes such as Horizon 2020, the European Commission's programme for boosting science and innovation, has become more attractive in a number of respects than North America, which is at risk of a brain-drain in the coming years. Regions such as California and Boston will remain exceptionally competitive and attractive, of course, but scientists are leaving for Asia, especially if they have family roots there. The change is perhaps even more evident among students, among whom students from Asia currently generate large incomes for universities in the US, Australia and England. They will increasingly remain in Asia, simply because the quality of the universities there will improve. This will deal a particularly heavy blow to university incomes, especially those universities that are sometimes entirely dependent for their income upon foreign students who are both willing and able to pay the high tuition fees.

In countries where economic contraction is occurring, this will certainly have consequences for the way in which universities offer expertise. Especially those in Europe, will be compelled to operate increasingly in a private market where demand plays a more decisive role than supply. In this sense, most European universities – which receive a relatively high level of government funding – are still largely supply-driven, and this will undoubtedly have to change. But there will also be a search for other forms of education, which are cheaper and perhaps just as effective. Digitization will bring great opportunities in this respect.

The shift in the economic balance, with all the consequences it will have, will be the most fundamental factor causing the university to change. Both global competition and the need to respond more keenly to social demand from students, among others, will compel universities to reassess ır priorities and structures. They will have to operate h less money in a more market-oriented, competitive way ın order to remain among the world's leading universities. This will ask a great deal of European universities, given that they are behind in the process of internationalization, but also in view of the relatively old-fashioned form of education they offer: a coherent curriculum, and not, as is the case in the Anglo-Saxon system, based on a range of what are largely separate courses. In view of the sharply rising cost of following a whole programme of study, demand for partial programmes, or even courses, will increase significantly. This process of fragmentation or 'unbundling' – increasingly offering separate 'knowledge packages' instead of complete programmes – will have a deep impact on the university.

Not only universities, but also governments will respond to the changing economic balance of power. When contraction occurs, the first reflex will be to focus on increasing economic returns, as happened in the Netherlands when the government steered research in the direction of the top sector agreements.[7] It would be a mark of vision if, in the coming years, governments were able to resist following their first instinct, but instead reflect more deeply on how to realize an affordable and future-proof system. When it comes to research, this could mean breaking up the uniform landscape in which all universities resemble one another, because only then will a system emerge that is able to respond to the many challenges. When it comes to teaching, it could mean taking a different approach to the enormous inflow of students who are all being squeezed through the same system. Instead, a system could be designed that guided students optimally to the place

7   See Chapter 6 for explanation of the Dutch science policy.

that was most suited to their talents. The future points to encouraging multiformity and differentiation whenever possible: in the Dutch context, the report of the Veerman Commission, which advised the government in 2010 on the future of higher education, remains just a relevant as it ever was.[8] It is a shame that the government seems to have forgotten this report.

8   Ministerie van Onderwijs, Wetenschappen en Cultuur, 2015: *Nederland 2035: trends en uitdagingen*. See also the report by the Veerman Commission, 2010, formally the Adviescommissie Toekomstbestendig Onderwijs [Advisory Commission on Future-Proof Education]: 'Differentiëren in drievoud'.

10. Urbanization and global knowledge hubs in 2040

The clichéd image of the university is one of a gathering of unworldly scholars who prefer to do their work in seclusion. In deep silence, research is conducted on subjects of which no one has ever heard, or might not even care about. Based on this picture, the ideal location for a university would be somewhere in a remote region, thereby guaranteeing these basic conditions of peace and seclusion. The question is: would it be possible to have a university at a great distance from social activity? Would it be desirable? Does the location of the university matter, and to what extent will universities in future be dependent on where they are located?

Walking around MIT in the US, or the campus of the Nanyang Technical University in Singapore, it is clear that these universities are closely connected with businesses or other social actors. There is no splendid isolation and there are no ivory towers. But the less technical top universities also maintain visible connections with social life, even if this is only because they are located in proximity to large cities that also have lively economic and financial sectors. Traditionally, universities have almost always been linked to cities that form economic and cultural centres. The fact that Harvard is now a top university has much to do with its location: for centuries, geographically close to America's economic and financial heart. In this way, every major city in Europe has or has had a university, and it is no accident that the most important universities are often linked to capital cities.

Nevertheless, something striking is going on. Since the rise of the World Wide Web, with all its potential for digital contact, there has been less need than ever to choose large cities, where the costs are high, in any case. But strangely enough, the importance of being located in a major city only seems to have increased in recent decades, even though distance is becoming less and less important for communication. Research carried out in Delft[1] confirms the increasing importance of being close to a metropolitan area. Moreover, it suggests that the nature and location of a campus play a defining role in the development of a university. How can this be the case, and how important is the city for the university?

The first and most obvious answer appears to lie primarily in the distance that students and staff are prepared to commute. To summarize, students prefer a lively metropolitan environment, with a nice campus close by that is equipped with every facility. The working conditions on campus and the attractiveness of the city are also key factors for talented academics, who are able to choose from a number of offers: the optimal situation is a university on a beautiful green campus, equipped with every convenience, in the neighbourhood of a large city with a broad cultural offering. In short: talent prefers the city for all the opportunities that the city can offer, and the university would be wise to follow this pattern in order to benefit from these opportunities, too.

There is a second, also self-evident factor. The size of the innovation pool is already now important, and will

1   See Den Heijer, A., 2011: *Managing the University*, Eburon Academic Publ.; See also Den Heijer, A. & G. Tzovlas, 2014: *The European Campus – Heritage and Challenges*, Delft University.

certainly remain so in future. Many studies suggest that the degree of innovation, which can be measured by the number of start-ups, for example, is dependent upon the metropolitan environment.[2,3] What is more, innovation is very good for the regional economy, but viewed the opposite way, an economy that is strongly focused on innovation is also very good for universities.

A third factor, indicated by the Dutch Scientific Council for Government Policy's incisive report *Towards a learning economy*, which includes an extensive comparison of the situations in different countries,[4] is the rapidly increasing importance of the 'knowledge ecosystem'. Although it might initially seem as such, the university does not function independently, but is connected to higher and vocational education colleges, hospitals, businesses and institutions of applied research, such as TNO in the Netherlands and Fraunhofer in Germany. The WRR has expanded this concept further, developing the image of knowledge dissemination in a regional system in which the generation of new knowledge and innovation is not linear, but circular. Only the metropolitan environment can provide enough fuel for such a close-knit and extensive knowledge system.

Singapore is a good example of a developed knowledge system such as this, in line with the WRR's observations. Due to logical and stimulating government policies, Singapore has five or so broader universities, in addition to a large

2   Shearmur, R., 2012: 'Are Cities the Front of Innovation? A Critical Review of the Literature on Cities and Innovation', *Cities*, vol. 29.

3   Lutao Ling, Fan Wang & Jian Li, 2016: 'Urban Innovation, Regional Externalities of Foreign Direct Investment and Industrial Agglomeration: Evidence from Chinese Cities', *Research Policies*, 830-843.

4   WRR (Wetenschappelijke Raad voor het Regeringsbeleid), 2013: *Naar een lerende economie. Investeren in het verdienvermogen van Nederland*, Amsterdam University Press (with English synopis).

ımber of institutions of higher professional and vocational ᴧJucation. The system is enriched by the many alliances that have been made with foreign institutions in the form of ASTAR (Agency for Science, Technology and Research) and CREATE institutions. The NUS is clearly the flagship university in the system, for which an incentive-based funding framework has been created. Having a top university such as the NUS is essential for a knowledge system like this, because this alone allows it to keep pace with developments at the forefront of science, which then radiate out to the other institutions. Based on these carefully orchestrated policies, it seems that Singapore will be able to face the competition in future.

The example of Singapore shows that what in economic geography is known to be true of large industrial centres could also be true of knowledge: a certain concentration of enterprise or knowledge and a degree of diversity are needed before a positive feedback loop starts working that ultimately leads to the emergence of large industrial or knowledge centres.[5] In the Netherlands, the 'Brainport' partnership in the Province of Brabant has benefitted from such a dynamic. Similar developments occurred in southern Finland and the Midlands in England. One might add that intriguingly, Berkeley is the only university in the world to date to have decided to attempt to create this dynamic on its own, thereby imitating Singapore. In the spring of 2015, Berkeley's vice chancellor, Nicholas Dirks, announced that a global campus would be built in the Richmond Bay Area that would welcome numerous top international institutions. In the Netherlands, other knowledge institutions are

5   Nomaler, Ö. & K. Frenken, 2014: 'On scaling of Scientific Knowledge Production in U.S. Metropolitan Areas'. *PLoS ONE*, 9.

often seen as competition, but the above suggests that it is smarter to see them as an enrichment of the local system, to which one can link oneself in order to achieve an optimal circulation of knowledge. Incidentally, it was announced in July 2016 that the Richmond Bay project has been called off and is at risk of failing due to a lack of funding, partly caused by the financial problems affecting the academic world as a whole.

Where will the knowledge hubs of the future be? And by 'knowledge hubs', here we mean concentrations of knowledge institutions that will play a leading, pioneering global role in the scholarship of the future. First, more than ever before, such hubs are being linked to global cities. As suggested above, this is related to the presence of sufficiently large pools of talent and innovation. This pattern has clearly taken shape in the US, where the East and West coasts in particular form the heart of the North American knowledge infrastructure. This is where one finds the most extensive networks of knowledge institutions, with the largest pools of talent, linked to the greatest funding potential for innovation.

In California, the whole Bay Area including Los Angeles can be seen as a hub, given the large number of top universities and other knowledge institutions linked to a very diverse, international and well-educated population, and lots of innovation. The region's impact is so great that there can be little doubt that by 2040 California will still be one of the large knowledge hubs, certainly in view of the old, but still effective, Master Plan for Higher Education that was designed to revitalize the whole system.[6] On the East Coast of the US we can identify such centres, those of Boston

6   *Times Higher Education*, 2016: 'The Californian System'. March 2016, 34-37.

and New York. Each has its own dynamic, but both have a great many public and private knowledge institutions, including some of the very best universities in the world. The concentration of large financial institutions in the two regions helps enormously, in particular when it comes to capitalizing on innovation. Despite the expected decline in the American system, North America will certainly be represented by these three hubs in 2040. By contrast, the chances of regions such as Chicago and Toronto developing into global hubs are much smaller, simply because there is an insufficient density of knowledge institutions and accompanying commercial activity.

It is expected that by 2040, Europe will have, at a maximum, the same number of knowledge hubs as North America, and probably fewer. There are few doubts that London and the surrounding region will remain a significant hub, although the Brexit vote also introduces uncertainty here. The presence of at least four top universities, plus the fantastic infrastructure of numerous other institutions, coupled with proximity to a strong financial centre, appears to guarantee London its position – certainly if the most recent developments are taken into account (such as the Francis Crick Institute, a partnership in the biomedical sciences, whereby 1,700 researchers from three top universities are working together). But after this, it becomes difficult. Most analyses identify Southern Germany plus the Zurich region as a likely candidate for developing into a second hub. Southern Germany is economically powerful and expanding, but there is no evidence of regional inter-linkage with Switzerland as of yet. Nevertheless, there is so much power in this region that it seems almost certain that there will also be a knowledge hub here by 2040. Greater uncertainty surrounds the regions of Copenhagen/Lund, Paris, and finally, the Randstad in the Netherlands. In the first and third cases, much depends on the conditions that are created to give them a push towards becoming worldwide hubs. Almost everyone considers France's chances to be small due to the prevailing educational system there, which grants little autonomy to institutions and lacks an internal dynamic.

The Netherlands and Belgium, along with North Rhine-Westphalia (including the Ruhr region) are very densely-populated urban areas without a metropolis with the allure of London or Paris. However, when you do the maths, you soon have 40-50 million people all together on a modest area of land characterised by a highly-educated population, a well-developed infrastructure and highly knowledge-intensive industry. In the western part of this area especially, in the Randstad conurbation predominantly (the area surrounding the four major cities of Amsterdam, The Hague, Rotterdam and Utrecht, which almost form a single conglomerate), and in the adjacent provinces of North Brabant and Flanders in the south, there will be many opportunities if the region is able to make better use of the mass of institutions by establishing smart partnerships. To start with, there are around twenty research-intensive universities in the Netherlands and Flanders, a large number of which are in the top hundred. There are also around seventy colleges of higher education, and all this in an area ($55,000 \text{ km}^2$) that is around a tenth of the size of California and that has around two-thirds of its population (23 million versus 38 million).

The density of universities is thus greater in the Netherlands and Flanders than in California, and the average level of education is certainly not worse, probably better. In other words, the potential is undoubtedly there, something that also becomes clear if we make the comparison with London: the region is comparable to the broad surroundings of the Greater London area in terms of area and population size, but the density of institutions in the Netherlands and Flanders is probably greater. The Randstad lacks real metropolitan cohesion,[7] however, and there is (still) a lack of genuinely top universities, which would be needed in order to form a global knowledge hub. The chances will improve if the Dutch system, possibly in cooperation with the Belgian one, were able to build better networks and a more effective knowledge ecosystem. Within the Dutch and Belgian area, this would most likely require the emergence of a number of larger nuclei, from which the more autonomous growth spiral of such a global hub could emerge.

When it comes to Asia, there is a high degree of concurrence among analysts. According to Kirby,[8] Korea and Japan are not in a position to move up to the top of the knowledge-institution ranking, perhaps with the exception of the fields of technology and medical technology. This seems related to the traditional orientation of these countries' knowledge institutions, which focus primarily on medicine and technology. This opinion appears to be confirmed by the developments of the last five years: although there is enough funding, particularly in Korea, even there the development of the universities is stagnating.

It seems very likely that in any case, Asia will be home to the following four knowledge hubs in 25 years' time: Beijing, Shanghai, Hong Kong/Shenzhen and Singapore. In the first three cases, these are mega-cities; in the case of Hong Kong

7   Xu, J. & QA.G.O. Yeh, 2011: *Governance and Planning of Mega-City Regions. An International Comparative Perspective*, Routledge Studies in Human Geography.
8   Kirby, W.C., 2014: 'The Chinese Century? The Challenges of Higher Education', *DAEDALUS*, Vol. 143, Spring 2014.

plus the surrounding regions and Shanghai, there is even a population of 50-100 million. Singapore presents a very different case in terms of the population size and thus the pool of talent, but many are nevertheless of the opinion that this region will function as a hub due to the sophisticated structure of its ecosystem.

It is striking that at present, there is much discussion in Asia of the Silk Road. It is clear that China is increasingly developing into a world power, regardless of what the Americans might think. But sustained Chinese economic growth is dependent upon having a large external consumer market, something that Europe can provide. China's leaders have therefore referred to the One-belt-one-road (Obor) a number of times in recent years as an example of how to link the two economic blocks, firstly via transport: research is being carried out into the potential of a high-speed train line between China and Europe. Following on from this, it has also been suggested that it would be an obvious move to link the European and Chinese knowledge systems in future. This would be less crazy than it sounds; the major Chinese universities have a growing interest in intensifying cooperation with Europe, also as a response to American foreign policy.

The universities themselves are powerless in the face of advancing urbanization, of course, and it is mainly governments that hold the reins of a number of relatively autonomous developments. In the Netherlands, for example, it is very important that we consider the Randstad and surrounding agglomerations as a single area, and that we encourage the creation of a truly national knowledge ecosystem. On a smaller scale, regional policy plays a particularly important role; in the long term, coherence between the knowledge institutions in each region forms an important basis for achieving connections at the national and supranational levels. This could be stimulated in a way comparable to how the government in Singapore encouraged the building of the knowledge economy: policy should be pursued not only with a view to funding the existing knowledge infrastructure, but also to stimulate the building of connections.

11. Information technology as a disruptive force

Morning rush hour at Hong Kong's Tsim Sha Tsui station: an enormous underground station where two metro lines intersect. A seething mass of people streams over the walkways to the exits or to connecting trains. All around, large signs proclaim: 'Look where you're going, not at your iPhone'. And the warning is pertinent: as they walk, 80% of the commuters are checking their email, holding face-time conversations, watching films, playing games, or sending text messages. There is no place with a higher density of iPhones, notebooks and laptops than the Hong Kong underground. Young people are constantly submerged in a digital world, whilst children aged three play with notebooks: one could hardly imagine a generation living a more virtual lifestyle! Based on this, one might assume that in Hong Kong, the digital university is just around the corner. But this is far from being the case; indeed, questions to this end are met with astonishment. Online courses and blended learning are all very well, but the campus university is as firmly established as ever – and there are good reasons for this.

The culture of Asian university education is characterized by having campuses with student houses, where the students often sleep four or more to a room. Imagine trying to find that in a Western country such as the Netherlands! Living on campus is seen as the norm, certainly in the first year and often in later years, too. This means that the character of Asian universities is often similar to that of universities in the US, with an active campus life. This is perceived as being very educational, certainly by parents, nd it is naturally an aspect that is lacking from the digital university. Secondly, people everywhere, but especially in Asian cultures, attach great importance to there being a visible relation between teacher and student. The professor, the teacher, is held in greater esteem than in the West, and cannot easily be replaced by an anonymous website or digital link. Although one should add that this is also one of the downsides to the Asian system, because many lecturers show little concern for their students, and the students often feel ignored by their lecturers. By contrast, even taking a few steps towards the digital university means that students can get a response to questions that they are still able to pose with a reasonable degree of anonymity.

All of this shows that the culture of teaching and research will have a far-reaching impact on the rapidity and degree to which the university will change under the influence of information technology. For something similar to that which applies to teaching applies to research, namely that physical proximity to other researchers and chats by the coffee machine are in fact important and are likely to remain so. In the short term, the influence of IT will therefore largely be felt in processes that relate to data storage and its use in various shifting relations. A trend will thereby continue that has already been taking shape for some time.

In the coming decades, the production and use of data will change in a manner that is comparable to that of the manufacturing of cars and aeroplanes. In the latter, all kinds of parts are produced in different places in the world before they are ultimately assembled in one location. In view of the ever-rising costs of scientific infrastructure, something similar will happen within the natural, medical and technical sciences. It is often simply not possible to have apparatus costing many millions of euros in a number of places. Shared use makes the facility affordable, and this will advance enormously with the increasing ease of data storage and transport. From the researcher's perspective the opposite is true, in the sense that the data are produced in different places in order to then bring them together.

The multiple use of large facilities sometimes leads to large groups of researchers who use parts of the same data files, which therefore need to be made sufficiently accessible. In the short term, the increasing use of data repositories such as these will be one of the most important developments, not only in the natural, medical and technical sciences, but also, for example, in the humanities, where large digital files are increasingly becoming available.

Data storage systems will become more important. The phenomenon of big data, whereby extremely large data files are searched and processed, will change the world of scholarship significantly, because the size of the files offers unprecedented opportunities for signal detection and reduction of background noise. Combining files from completely different disciplines also presents an opportunity for major breakthroughs, which are in fact no longer limited by the technological possibilities, due to having increasingly powerful computers.

All of these possibilities will certainly promote so-called 'convergences', amalgamations of different disciplines that use totally different data and methodologies. Large breakthroughs can still be expected here, because these combinations will in essence open up new fields of research.[1] This includes

1   National Research Council, 2014: *Convergence. Facilitating Transdisciplinary Integration of Life Sciences, Physical Sciences, Engineering, and Beyond*, The National Academies Press.

combinations of medical-technological disciplines, but also disciplines that lie much further apart, such as urban development and health, where all kinds of data on people's living situations and movement are linked to health and vitality.

There is yet another development that could lead to a significant breakthrough in online knowledge, and this is illustrated by mass public participation in a number of research projects. These 'citizen science projects'[2] often involve the gathering of robust data on certain phenomena, such as the nature of climate change. Although they are not yet very visible, citizen science projects may lead to real change in future, as they involve the accumulation of enormous numbers of observations: in this respect, too, the big data phenomenon is facilitating completely new forms of research.

Finally, we can expect major developments in the way in which scholarly results are published and made available. Much recent literature, including the powerfully expressed posts on a recent blog,[3] shows that the whole system of quality control by colleagues, the so-called peer review system, is failing when it comes to detecting insufficient quality, errors and sometimes even fraud. Alternatives to this control process are starting to emerge, which include, for example, making a draft paper available on the Internet at an early stage, so that it can be criticized by colleagues and screened for errors. This is an almost 'wiki-like' form of quality control that is highly dependent upon IT, whereby in principle, the whole scholarly community can participate in monitoring quality, rather than a very small group.

2   LERU Advice Paper 20, 2016: 'Citizen Science at Universities: Trends, Guidelines and Recommendations'.

3   Belluz, J., B. Plumer & B. Resnick, July 2016: The 7 Biggest Problems Facing Science, According to 270 Scientists, Vox.com.

This change in the review process means that it now takes much less time to make data available. Whereas in the past it could sometimes take a year or more before an article appeared in print, the use of digital journals means that this process can be accelerated more often. A further step will entail the emergence of a growing circuit of 'grey' articles, namely articles that have not gone through an independent quality review by colleagues. This will not only save time, but will also increasingly allow academics to avoid the barriers used by journals, whereby articles can often only be read after the publisher has been paid via a subscription or per-article charge. Open publishing is completely in line with the trend towards open science, which involves making scientific findings accessible to the public on a broad, open basis.

All in all, our focus should perhaps not be primarily on the growth of digital knowledge transfer in teaching and the digital university, but on a very different phenomenon. Perhaps the disruptive innovation is not IT technology for the exchange of knowledge via massive open online courses (MOOCs), but the rise of big data and, with this, the massification of teaching and research. In the context of teaching, this would suggest that MOOCs are not the final outcome of the change, but rather an intermediary phase in the long-term move towards a global teaching pool with new forms of teaching[3] and new forms of certification, comparable to the role of big data and citizen science in research. If this is true, in any case, this will demand very different qualities from students from the ones they currently have: at present, the students' lecturer determines what is to be learned, and the students follow the lecturer. Students will shortly have to find their way through an enormous range of knowledge and teaching material, and lecturers will go from being gurus to guides.

It is clear that IT will fundamentally change the landscape of higher education. Although at present, the change is mainly visible in products such as MOOCs, the transformation will cut much deeper. Knowledge will soon be omnipresent: not only something to be gleaned from a book in the library, but available everywhere, all the time. Knowledge will thereby become fluid: formalized knowledge in books and publications will be transformed into a wiki-like knowledge base, consisting both of formalized knowledge that has been assessed properly in relation to its quality, and also so-called 'grey knowledge' whose quality has not yet been assessed. It will be possible to use and combine knowledge in rapidly changing ways, and the rate of circulation of knowledge will become much shorter. Whilst at present it takes a year to go from manuscript to publication, this process will soon become much quicker, and the time that the knowledge remains relevant will likewise be cut due to its mass production.

Faced by this compelling innovation in the availability of knowledge, universities and governments often look to the power of technology: more and larger systems, more and improved animations, more and improved serious games. This is a tempting response, in view of the opportunities that are on offer. But it is at least equally important that the university and government should continue to invest in the development of originality and creativity, in both teaching and research. In future, these will continue to be the vital distinguishing features of pioneering scholarship.

12. Digital or campus teaching?

What opportunities does the digital university offer, as seen by today's universities, and what are the implications of information technology for education? The university with the longest tradition in this area is MIT, which has been running so-called OpenCourseWare online since 2002. The project started under the leadership of Robert Brown, the then provost of MIT; officially, the project was motivated by a desire to encourage international cooperation by means of distance learning. Behind this, however, lay the idea of the shared intellectual commons, offering knowledge in the global commons in a way comparable to shared use of the 'commons', the common land, in the Middle Ages. Based on this mix of commercial interests and idealism, MIT has put large amounts of open course material on the Internet since 2002, and this has proved a hit. At present, 2,260 courses are available, and the site has had 175 million visitors to date![1] Few institutions have benefited so greatly from making a generous gesture: worldwide brand awareness has risen enormously and societal support for the university has risen even further.

It appeared that the MOOC would become the twenty-first century's great disruptive technology in the education sector. The MOOC is a form of teaching in which large numbers of students can participate, often from many different countries and frequently lacking the formal prior qualifications demanded in admissions requirements. The first MOOC dates from 2008. In the same spirit as MIT's

---

1   Roth, Michael S., 2014: *Beyond the University. Why Liberal Education Matters*, Yale University Press.

OpenCourseWare, it was intended as an attempt to offer a service to society and democratize education, in the sense of broadening social participation. The major breakthrough came in 2011, with Stanford University's MOOC on artificial intelligence. The fact that 160,000 people took part drew attention from around the world, and it was mainly the huge PR value and the attention that Stanford received from society that gave a massive boost to this form of education. Nowadays there are hundreds of MOOCs (most of them still based in the US), and there are a number of commercial platforms that provide MOOCs and make them accessible.

Until now, the consequences of the IT revolution for higher education have seemed limited. No one disputes the importance of blended learning and the sharply growing impact of IT on knowledge transfer. But almost everyone believes that MOOCs stand no chance as a self-contained educational innovation: the peak of the hype appears to be over and the business model has proved untenable.[2] The cost of producing MOOCs cannot be met or can only partly be met by the returns, whereby the value to society is pretty much all that remains. Despite this, Harvard and MIT are continuing to invest heavily in MOOCs and other forms of digital knowledge transfer. Why are they doing so, if it is clear to everyone that this approach has no commercial prospects?

There are nevertheless a few signs that indicate broader opportunities for massive online participation than those suggested above. Michael Roth, president of Wesleyan University in Connecticut, the US, describes the university's MOOC on 'The modern and postmodern' as a success,

2   McPherson, M.S. & L.S. Bacow, 2015: 'Online Higher Education: Beyond the Hype-Cycle'. *J. Econ, Perspectives*, 29, 135-154.

despite the large number of drop-outs, on the grounds that it created a truly international classroom with unprecedented reach among extremely motivated and inspired students.[1] Above all, it shed a wholly new light on the university's own education: for once, not education for a highly select, very homogenous group of Wesleyan students, but for a group of exceptionally diverse and extremely motivated students who contributed entirely new opinions. The university's teaching took on a totally new dimension, approaching the old American ideal of knowledge for all: the notion that the university is responsible for democratizing knowledge. This is often felt more keenly in America than in Europe, and will certainly help to give further impetus to online education.

There is a second motivation for this online education: it is striking that 80% of MIT students are already using a wide range of MOOCs, while the university's 'own' teaching material is playing a more minor role, certainly in the undergraduate phase. Here we can see a clear trend towards a global education pool, whereby the emphasis is shifting from local teaching material to a network of courses spanning the whole world. Knowledge is literally becoming a globalized, mass phenomenon: following a MOOC given by a Harvard professor, a student from MIT will chat with students in Singapore, China and Australia, before passing his MIT exams with only limited instruction from his own lecturer. And in addition to geographical spread, online education also offers the possibility of distribution across age: MOOCs and lifelong learning were made for each other, as flexible decisions can be made per course as to how to meet an individual's learning needs over their lifetime or career.

Officially, Harvard, Berkeley, Stanford and MIT remain utterly convinced by the utility of the MOOC: hundreds of millions of dollars have been invested, and the official line is that this will continue in the coming years. Conversations behind the scenes make it clear, however, that there are also doubts here about the tenability of this form of digital education. The strategy is shifting towards the use of a mixed model that is roughly as follows: OpenCourseWare will continue to exist and many digital courses will retain an 'open' element, but the share of 'closed' courses will also grow. The best lecturers will provide the public courses, which will form an attractive, high-quality element in a pool of modules that will be accessible to a wide audience. This pool will be of great importance to smaller universities and colleges that are unable to produce their own online courses, and will thus collaborate on this with the producing universities. In this way, a network will emerge of producing and consuming universities and colleges, in which not only OpenCourseWare and MOOCs play a role, but also closed courses are made available to the network on an exclusive basis, in the form of SPOCs (small personal online courses), for example.

At present, most investment in the combination of open and closed digital courses described above is taking place in the US and Northwestern Europe. But a pool of digital resources, open or closed, will only work and will only be profitable if there are multiple users. It is therefore essential to build a good network. Over time, the growth of these networks will mean that education takes place within largely closed, partly open networks and platforms. This will mean a fall in the cost for participants, whereas for universities, it is clear that the key will be to join the right network at the right time.

Although the digital university, as of yet, is not threatening the classical university in Asia, in the US, this is the case.

Why is this so? The answer is likely to be a simple one: price! Tuition fees in the US are much higher than in Asia. And as a result, the balance in the US is rapidly shifting in the direction of the virtual university, where one can get a degree for much less money than at the average American university – one of the hundreds of anonymous public colleges and public universities. For these latter universities, the digital university will undoubtedly become a formidable competitor.[3] This development will not threaten the Ivy League, however: people with money or unbridled faith in their own future will still be prepared to pay exorbitant tuition fees for highly selective degree programmes, in the expectation that this will guarantee them a good job. It is a question of having faith in getting a good return on one's investment.

The rapid advance of the digital university in the US may form an acute threat to the public universities, which deliver a rather mediocre level of education for a considerable price in the form of high, and still rising, tuition fees. It is clear that with a further hike in fees, the balance of cost versus quality will soon tip in favour of the digital university (if this has not already happened). But digital education may have a second, and possibly even more drastic, effect on education in general: will campus education still exist in future, or is a more radical 'unbundling' or fragmentation occurring? The latter is already observable in the trend towards modularization, in the form of self-standing educational modules, even without the immediate intention of gaining a degree. Unbundling makes it much easier to follow tailor-made education, such as by following only

3   For a similar view, see: Barber, M., K. Donnelly & S. Rizvi, 2013: *An Avalanche Is Coming. Higher Education and the Revolution Ahead*, Institute for Public Policy Research.

those courses in which one has an interest at that time. Such a development is inconceivable in the Northwestern European system at present, because the latter is highly focused on providing degrees for a whole curriculum, but it is already much more common in the American system.

Almost everyone agrees that campus education will still exist for the top layer of universities in 25 years' time. In making this claim, people frequently – and probably correctly – point to the educational benefit of studying in a community: the essential interaction with peers in the form of actual face-to-face education. This is mainly true of the 'foundational' phase of a programme, the initial years of university education. Online teaching may well increase significantly during this phase, but the continued existence of the physical campus will not be threatened.

After these first two years of study at university, however, there is a substantial chance of continued 'unbundling': less campus education and more distance learning. After a period on campus of one or two years, students will enter the labour market, possibly while studying further for a Bachelor's degree via distance learning. The societal value of the Bachelor's degree will decrease and might be partially replaced by in-company learning.[3] In this vision of the future, only in the best research universities will there be continued interest in gaining a full Bachelor's degree via on-campus learning, although this will only be the case if this can offer demonstrable added value in comparison to digital providers. This added value could come in the form of intensive training in research skills (fieldwork and lab work), professional skills (medicine, law or governance), or interaction with fellow students that also focuses on preparation for a Master's or doctoral degree, thus as part of an intensive research career.

All in all, IT will undoubtedly play an exceptionally powerful driving role in the changes that are going to affect higher education.[4,5] We should not forget that we have just 25 years of experience in this area, and these developments have already had a far-reaching impact; it is inevitable that we will see at least as many changes in the coming years.

4   The NMC Horizon Report, 2016: *Higher Education Edition*.
5   Ernst & Young, 2012: *University of the Future – A Thousand Year Old Industry on the Cusp of Profound Change*.

13. The labour market and lifelong learning

In recent decades, there has been a sharp rise in the proportion of graduates in the labour force, mainly in Western countries. Whereas there were 424,000 students in the Netherlands in 1990, by 2015 this had already risen to 664,000, an increase of 56%. Most OECD countries have seen similar increases. In view of this, it is striking that in the same period, the US slipped from first to thirteenth place in terms of the share of highly educated people in the population.[1] In other words, although the West has seen a significant rise in the proportion of graduates, the pattern differs sharply from country to country. Nevertheless, on paper, every government is following policies that are designed to encourage such an increase. This follows from the idea that a high-quality economy that is characterized by a high level of innovation is dependent upon having a highly educated workforce. In addition to governments encouraging rising participation in tertiary education, there is a second and extremely important reason for the growing influx of students: access to better paid segments of the job market is now largely determined by having a university degree.

In countries in Asia, South America and Africa, there has likewise been a sharp increase in the number of people attending higher education.[2] China alone has around 2,500

---

1   See the OECD figures and commentary on them in Crow, Michael M. & William B. Dabars, 2015: *Designing the New American University*, Johns Hopkins University Press.

2   *Times Higher Education*, 2016: 'With Greater Participation even "Greater" Inequality'. June, 20-21.

universities and colleges of higher education, and invests 250 billion dollars a year in human capital.[3] It is predicted that by 2020, 195 million people will have attended higher education, and yet we can already see the first signs that there is not enough employment for all university graduates. This points to a growing problem: whereas on the one hand, governments are choosing to build 'knowledge economies', on the other, there is a growing mismatch between demand and supply in the labour market. A large number of countries already have an over-supply of graduates and an under-supply of manufacturing staff, whilst the middle segment of the labour market is being eroded due to robotization and computerization.[3]

Governments' efforts to create knowledge economies are grounded in the expectation that such economies are by and large characterized by innovation and services, which in turn leads to rising levels of prosperity. This means that in addition to direct investment in education, it is also very important to have indirect investment. This investment in various kinds of knowledge capital, often private ones, has been shown to be indicative of the future strength of the economy: this can include software and data, new intellectual property and services, and investment in brand awareness and staff training.[4] All wealthy countries have a high proportion of this kind of knowledge capital, whereby the economy is pushed further in the direction of the knowledge economy over time. Due to the government's encouragement of participation in higher education, supported by students' desire to enter the better-paid segments of the labour market, the economy

3   Ministerie van Onderwijs, Wetenschappen en Cultuur, 2015: *Nederland 2035: trends en uitdagingen*.
4   See the 2011 OECD report in: Ministerie van Onderwijs, Wetenschappen en Cultuur, 2015: *Nederland 2035: trends en uitdagingen*.

gradually shifts in the direction of the knowledge economy, further prompted by private knowledge capital, whereby a spiral emerges. At the same time, the importance of the manufacturing sector declines as these businesses relocate to other parts of the world, attracted by low wages and an adequate supply of skilled manufacturing employees.

It is clear that in addition to the shifts that are occurring under the influence of education policy, the labour market will change radically as a result of robotization and computerization. Existing analyses show that the middle segment of the labour market is being eroded and will shrink significantly in terms of the supply of labour.[5] Tasks that computers and robots are not yet able to do, such as tasks that include a highly creative element, tend to be located in the higher segment of the labour market and will not be affected for now. But in future, a very different labour market will emerge across the world; one with a strongly polarized character, with shrinking employment prospects for the middle segment.

In summary, we see the following picture emerging: participation in higher education will continue to grow strongly in the coming years, because governments are pursuing policies that are designed to stimulate the knowledge economy. There are limits to this, however: we can already see the first signs of structural unemployment in the highly-educated segment, because the middle segment

5   See Frey, C.B. & M.A. Osborne, 2013: *The Future of Employment. How Susceptible Are Jobs to Computerization?*, Oxford Martin Publications. For a similar analysis, see the report by the Dutch Advisory Council on Government Policy/WRR (Went et al., 2015), which makes an emphatic case for allowing education to play a role in preparing for a 'robotized future'. See also *The Future of the Professions* by Susskind and Susskind (2014), in which it is argued that not only the middle segment of the labour market is under threat, but also the professions, such as those of doctor, lawyer and consultant.

of the labour market is being eroded and there are fewer opportunities for the graduates trying to avoid this. At the same time, there is falling interest in working the manufacturing sector in jobs that require a lower level of education; a sector that, moreover, is shifting to low-wage countries on the basis of cost, among other factors.

These developments are causing a growing mismatch between supply in the labour market and opportunities for university graduates. Partly due to this, countries such as India are already taking measures to limit access to higher education via more selective admissions. In Hong Kong and Mainland China, every university has an annual quota that prevents the number of highly educated people from soaring too high. The US and England also have selective systems and high tuition fees, which may help to limit the mismatch. However, it is in countries with unlimited access to higher education, such as the Netherlands or Germany and Scandinavia, where the mismatch with the job market will be greatest, certainly if a country decides not to compensate for the erosion of the middle segment of the job market. A social division will then emerge, with a large supply of graduates and possibly unemployment at the top of the job market, a shrinking middle class, due to erosion of the middle section of the job market, and finally, a shrinking manufacturing sector that has seen work transferred elsewhere, drawn by low wages. The net outcome will be that the labour market has less and less space for compensation and displacement. Across the world, the division into knowledge countries and manufacturing countries is becoming more entrenched, but there is a mismatch with the labour market in both types of economy.

Lifelong learning can play an important role in resolving these mismatches. Depending on the country and the system in which a university finds itself, in future, students may choose a university or programme only then to conclude that they are not adequately equipped for the job market. Certainly, in cases where a government has not placed limits on the influx of students or taken labour demand into account in admissions policy, and where the mismatch with the job market is potentially greatest, retraining or additional training via lifelong learning could offer a solution. One should add, though, that lifelong learning means much more than retraining or on-the-job training: it is an answer to students' demands for 'tailor-made' or even personalized education.

We can expect to see increasing demand for differentiation and made-to-measure education not only from students, but also from the labour market. In a study published in 2013 (*An avalanche is coming*), Michael Barber and colleagues[6] emphasized that shorter, modularized study programmes with tailored content, followed by further professional training, could become the new form of education. This opinion is shared by the futurist Ross Dawson.[7] Whereas the system is now geared towards graduates with four or five years of higher education, it is clear that people will soon be entering the labour market more quickly and may well complete their training later, via lifelong learning, if the labour market demands this. In a real knowledge economy, in future it will increasingly be about not only the share of highly-educated people, but perhaps even more so, the question of how these highly-educated people will be able

6   Barber, M., K. Donnelly & S. Rizvi, 2013: *An Avalanche Is Coming. Higher Education and the Revolution Ahead*, Institute for Public Policy Research.
7   Dawson, R.: *The Future of Universities*. http://rossdawson.com/keynote-speaker/keynote-speaking-topics/keynote-speaking-topics-the-future-of-universities-and-education/#ixzz3Sm37jL1q.

to respond flexibly to demand from the labour market. In this sense, the demand for retaining and additional training that comes from practice ('problem-driven learning'; see Dawson) may well form a much better commercial foundation for lifelong learning than the need for general self-development that has formed the key basis until now. Judging from the fate of open universities worldwide, this latter approach has had only mediocre results.

The above gives rise to a picture of growing demand for lifelong learning, but mainly in the context of customized and problem-solving education. In relation to this, Smidt and Sursock[8] refer to 'the engaged university'; a type of university that uses lifelong learning, among other things, to extend the concept of higher education, as they put it, 'to enable higher education to demonstrate value beyond the "ivory tower"'. Later in their argument, they observe that the strength of universities can lie in the fact that they offer education and research 'using real-life problems and issues, and engaging in research that is derived and developed in tandem with end-users. This ensures that research promotes social, economic, and technological innovation in a reciprocal partnership...'

The suggestion that the university of the future should become more engaged resembles Goddard's argument for a civic university,[9] in which the university identifies more closely with societal problems and developments on every front. And it is likely that the problems in 2040 will be

8   Smidt, H. & A. Sursock, 2011: *Engaging in Lifelong Learning: Shaping Inclusive and Responsive University Strategies*. EUA (European University Association) publications 2011.

9   Goddard, J. & P. Vallance, 2011: 'The Civic University: Re-uniting the University and the City', *Higher Education in Cities and Regions: For Stronger, Cleaner and Fairer Regions*. OECD, Paris.

massive, even compared with today's already significant problems: without a change in policy, the still-growing global population will put heavy pressure on the supply of raw materials, and distributing scarce resources will become a problem of the first order, all the more so as wealthy countries will have to become more accommodating in relation to developing countries, which will first ask for and may then demand their share. In addition to the scarcity of raw materials, there will be the growing problem of scarce energy and food to maintain a global population of what will soon be around nine billion people. This, too, mainly entails far-reaching distribution problems, because on balance the world does have enough food and energy, but it is currently used and distributed in an extremely unequal way. Future scenarios for food and energy production will be complicated even further by the enormous migration to the city and the development of existing cities into megacities. Agriculture in the city, the consumption of meat at a high cost, and ensuring the availability of sufficient clean water are all problems that will increasingly need to be addressed. It is expected that these future problems will occur in the context of considerable climate change that may be virtually irreversible. In addition to the warming of the entire earth and rising sea levels, this may also have far-reaching consequences in the form of flooding and water shortages, the availability of food, and may also bring risks to public health.

The engaged university will have to deal with all of these problems. They are problems that will require technological innovation in order to develop new products and solutions. In addition, however, in many respects, the future will also be about how to redistribute scarce resources, and to achieve stable forms of governance that guarantee sufficient raw rials and food for large parts of the world population. se are not technological problems but sociological es; problems to which the social sciences and humanities are particularly good at contributing solutions. The engaged university will provide these disciplines with new opportunities. However, the complexity of the problems will also require, to an increasing extent, academically trained people who are able to perceive the connections between problems and think across the disciplines. This is the essence of the T-shaped professional: a well-trained graduate who can draw on a strong disciplinary training (the vertical part of the 'T') to form broad connections with other disciplines in order to develop joint solutions (the horizontal bar of the 'T').

14.   The civic university

People in Asia respond with amazement when asked what the university is actually for; in other words, what they understand the mission of the classical university to be.[1,2] The debate on this question in Europe and in the US barely exists in Asia. Teaching and research belong in every university model, of course; but the Asian tradition is very different from the European or American one, and it is important to take this into account when thinking about the future development of the university.

Traditionally, education in Asia took place in a very different context from that of the university, a typically European Renaissance invention that originally had a highly professional character. The university as we know it today has only existed in China for one hundred years.[3] It was preceded by Tong Shi education, which revolved around learning from the past in the Confucian tradition. This was a strong liberal tradition, in the sense that it provided a free scientific education with a broad humanistic basis. This approach fits seamlessly with the modern teaching of liberal arts and sciences, which is why the latter was embraced by some Chinese universities with a striking degree of rapidity and ease.

There are fundamental differences between the traditional Chinese Tong Shi system and the modern university.

1   Verbrugge, A., J. van Baardwijk, (eds), 2014: *Waartoe is de universiteit op aarde?*, Boom.

2   King, G. & M. Sen, 2013: 'The Troubled Future of Colleges and Universities', *Political Science and Politics*, 46, 81-113.

3   *International Higher Education*, 2015: 'Special 20th Anniversary Feature: Higher Education's Future. Spring 2015.

To start with, in modern China the state plays a key role in regulating the university and shaping the programmes that prioritize science and engineering. According to the Beijing Consensus, the government's aim, by playing a central role, is to contribute as efficiently as possible to the acceleration of economic growth. This has completely dominated the formidable growth of Chinese universities, whereby the state, if needs be, reassumes control of the universities if its objectives have not been met. Whereas the level of academic freedom that exists in Europe and the US is seriously in question here, until now, this has been accepted in China without a murmur.

The situation is not so very different in other Asian countries: Singapore, Hong Kong, Korea and other countries have what are in fact very recent, modern universities, which are often structured along the lines of the British model. The structure is usually the only similarity, however: most universities have a strong focus on technology and innovation, although with growing prosperity in recent decades, there has been a tendency within the best universities to pay more attention to the humanities and social sciences. As the above already suggests, the role of the Asian universities is still largely to educate high-quality workers in a way that is closely tailored to demand from the labour market, as well as having a key focus on research: this is the basic mission for countries that are developing, and will undoubtedly remain so in future.

Even more so than in the western societies, in the coming years Asian, South American and African universities will act as vehicles for social mobility and gateways to good jobs. The rationale of the university will thereby largely be economic: investment has to deliver demonstrable returns. Only with rising prosperity will space open up for the humanities and the social sciences, which are harder to justify directly in economic terms. Arguments such as that advanced by Collini, who justifies investing in the university on the grounds of cultural and other interests rather than economic ones, will hardly be addressed in the coming years. Even in a country like Japan, the faculties of social sciences and humanities were recently closed in 26 of the 60 state universities on the orders of the Minister of Education.[4] The latter called on universities to take 'active steps to abolish [social science and humanities] organizations or to convert them to serve areas that better meet society's needs'.

With shrinking budgets in Europe and the US, however, simple views such as that of John Adams, the second president of the US – 'The whole people must take upon themselves the education of the whole people, and must be willing to bear the expense of it' – will also be endorsed less and less. There, too, the university will have to face economic realities and find out what is still acceptable in light of its core values and other responsibilities, and how much this will cost, for example, in terms of its independence and autonomy.

What will form the core basis for the university's existence in 25 years' time? During a meeting of the League of European Research Universities (LERU) in Geneva in 2015, three speakers voiced, rather coincidentally, totally different visions. Micheline Calmy-Rey is the former president of the Swiss Confederation and played a key role in the Geneva region. In Geneva, she was responsible for finance, and she

---

4   *Times Higher Education*, 2015: 'Social Sciences and Humanities Faculties "to Close" in Japan after Ministerial Intervention. Universities to Scale Back Liberal Arts and Social Science Courses'. September 2015.

brought the budget for the canton of Geneva back on track with a relatively heavy hand. This budget covers the University of Geneva, because some universities in Switzerland are financed by the cantons. When she was directly responsible for finance, Calmy-Rey always protected the education budget. Her view in this regard is very simple: education is always priority number one, because only education can give people real opportunities for the future. The objection that the rising cost of healthcare, for example, means that sacrifices will inevitably have to be made in education – and thus in the universities – always provoked the same response on her part: there is nothing as important for the future of a people and of a nation as education.

During the meeting, a second vision was outlined by the former president of the European Commission, José Manuel Barroso. Barroso has since become a professor in Geneva and also has a position at Princeton, in addition to what is probably a considerable number of other roles. He spoke before and during the dinner, mainly on the differences between the universities in the US and Europe. The core of his argument was that there is very little innovation in Europe, whereas universities in the US are more dynamic and the relationship with industry is much stronger. To a certain extent, he blamed European universities for this, because American universities, in his view, are more entrepreneurial and thus more willing to enter into partnership with industry. However, he thereby passed too rapidly over the American tradition of government and industry investing considerably more in applied research. Moreover, as we have frequently mentioned above, there is an even more compelling reason for American universities to be entrepreneurial: the sharply reduced contribution from government.

Barroso was actually making a different point, however: he was arguing that a great many new developments have been, and will be, spurred on by applied research, meaning that the scientific dynamic in American universities, more so than in Europe, is partly nurtured by innovation. He added that this is good for universities, as they then draw more support from society, and good for society, which values the university as a result, rather than seeing it as ballast.

The third speaker was Michael Møller, director general of the United Nations in Geneva. He emphasized that the world is changing radically. State power and authority is fragmenting wherever one looks, and we still lack new forms of governance. As the state fragments, we face rapidly growing problems that cross borders and even continents. Significant shifts in land-use are bound up with the climate problem, whilst at the same time there is a distressing lack of water and food. In addition, there is a shortage of metals and raw materials, which will undoubtedly lead to serious confrontations between the different economic blocks as they attempt to secure stocks of raw materials. In this context, Møller argued, academia must play a role by carrying out fundamental and applied research in order to find real, innovative solutions.

These three visions, advanced in a single day in May 2015, cover the whole spectrum of ways in which the modern university can be justified. In the first place, Calmy-Rey, who takes the most traditional view and emphasizes the university's intrinsic value: knowledge liberates every individual, because knowledge brings unprecedented opportunities. The conservation and cultivation of knowledge form the basis for a well-functioning society that is able to solve problems, and centres of knowledge should thus lie at the heart of a society. This vision leaves no room for doubt: like John Adams, Calmy-Rey believes the preservation of the university to be an essential state task that should be carried out without question and has virtually no limits. When asked about the state's return on its investment, her answer is not expressed in economic terms, but, as above, couched in terms of the limitless possibilities that knowledge offers.

Barroso's vision emphasizes a very different benefit that the university can bring: knowledge must be made to pay in terms of innovation. Even more so, innovation and interaction with society makes the university better and more creative, and it also increases support for the university within society by making knowledge pay. This is a straightforward plea for a more entrepreneurial university. Although John Adams might have viewed this with concern, because Barroso's argument is rooted firmly in a demand for economic returns, Barroso's reasoning is more complex and perhaps more reassuring than many scholars might think. Indeed, there are very good examples of creative innovations that bring excellent economic returns, and these undoubtedly increase political support for investment in universities. Moreover, it cannot be denied that some innovations have boosted innovation in scholarship: one need only think of the rise of social media and the changes that have accompanied this in computer science, for example.

Michael Møller puts a third element on the table, one that at first sight resembles Barroso's vision, but that on closer inspection is something completely different: Møller is making the case for all of the university's knowledge to be put at the service of solving major social problems. This is not about curiosity-driven teaching and research, nor about valorization in an economic sense; instead, it is about returns in terms of social capital. In the light of the massive problems that are looming, often on a global scale, and given the drama that has played out in recent decades in relation to climate change, food supplies and the erosion of the political system, Møller is asking, in plain terms, for universities to make a great effort in order to find solutions.

In the coming 25 years, justifying the university will not be as straightforward as it was in Von Humboldt's day. We can expect a modern university that forms part of society to be subject to demands for economic justification and returns, certainly in an age when governments have to make tough choices. Above all, though, it seems that there is an urgent need for the university to take its social responsibilities more seriously, on the grounds that the knowledge it possesses is not meant for a limited number of stakeholders in society, such as students or private actors who are willing to pay for it, but should also be used to solve the major problems that affect society.

In an overview of the different types of universities, Barnett,[5] too, argues that universities have an essential role to play in society. The university is no longer an ivory tower that produces knowledge for itself, nor a professional firm that produces knowledge for its own benefit. Barroso's model of the entrepreneurial university is also untenable. The university of the future will derive its right to exist primarily from being active *in* the world and by producing knowledge *for* the world.

---

5   Barnett, R., 2011: *Being a University*, Routledge.

Part 3
Contours of the university of the future

What will the university's mission be in the year 2040? How will the university be funded, and what kind of teaching and research will be needed? Will campus universities still exist? These are all issues on which universities will have to make fundamental choices in the coming years. A new university will emerge that, like the one of today, will need constant legitimization in society: certainly, we should not take its continued existence for granted. Although some fundamental values will remain unchanged, we need to reflect on new core values, in view also of rapidly changing societal circumstances. In order to maintain a strong system, the university will also need to engage in ongoing debate with the government, for there will be a high level of differentiation among universities in the system, varying from what will sometimes be narrow teaching universities to comprehensive research universities. In the ideal case, connected ecosystems will emerge that encompass other knowledge institutions, in which the university will be able to play a central role. Distance learning will increase as a result of advancing digitization, and, with this, the need for tailored education. In addition, less value will be attached to the final degree certificate, and lifelong learning will become more important. As part of all these changes, it is crucial that the university focus on more than knowledge transfer alone: it is about making a meaningful contribution to society, striving for wisdom rather than for knowledge. Hopefully the university will achieve a completely different role from that which is portrayed in the classical image of the ivory tower: at the heart of society, as a guide that leads the debate, speaking with authority on major questions in a world ruled by the wisdom of the crowd – in what, since Brexit and the US elections, has been called the 'post-fact society'.

15. *Quid durat?*

How easily will universities be able to adapt and how rapidly will a new course be set? The magnitude of the challenges associated with creating the university of the future, based on its current form and traditions, becomes clear when one pays a visit to an American Ivy League university. It is a beautiful day, 28 May 2015, seven o'clock in the morning: Harvard Yard and the whole Harvard University campus is full of chairs. There is room for 37,000 people, and it is hard to imagine that all these chairs will be occupied in the course of the morning. But the first signs that this will happen are already plain to see: in the week before Commencement Day (graduation day), Cambridge becomes busier, boards with slogans such as 'Congratulations to all our Graduate Students' appear in the shops and hotels, the hotels are booked up and the somewhat sleepy atmosphere of the town is transformed. There is a palpable sense of excitement, and all kinds of activities are held in the days leading up to Commencement Day.

Some of the things that are happening are likely to bewilder European visitors, who have a more down-to-earth perspective: the pomp and circumstance, the pathos and academic symbolism are not exactly suggestive of the university of the future. At half past seven the campus is already pretty busy, and there are people up and about in all of the old buildings (also old in European terms; with a bit of fancy footwork, Harvard can be said to date back to 1636, and many of the buildings date from between the seventeenth and the nineteenth centuries). At a quarter to eight, the graduates and fellows, preceded by bagpipes players, make their way to a church service that begins at eight o'clock sharp, attended by the president of the university and the provost.

At half past eight the alumni form their own procession, marking the beginning of an endless stream of processions from the different buildings: together with the alumni, graduates dressed in black (Bachelor's and Master's) or red (PhDs) move to the central area and all of the other chairs also slowly fill with family and visitors. The alumni are preceded by the oldest members, the class of 1941, meaning that the oldest alumnus present is in his nineties. At a quarter to ten sharp, the morning's activities begin, in which the degree certificates are awarded.

The word 'commencement' is derived from *inceptio*, a Latin term used in the Middle Ages to describe the ceremony at which candidates were admitted to the degree of Master and were given a licence to teach (similar to for example the Belgian *licentiaat*). The morning is a celebration of the graduates who have achieved the three types of degree: Bachelor's, Master's and doctoral. The Master's degree logically indicates the first phase of higher learning, which allows the student to go on to prepare for the doctorate. Hardly anyone joins the procession for this degree, aside from a relatively small group who are ending their studies at this point. The great majority of graduates are Bachelor's, and the largest groups are from the Harvard Liberal Arts and Sciences College, the School of Business, and the School of Law, respectively. In contrast to Europe where the majority of students finish their academic education with a Master's degree, here most will finish with this Bachelor's degree and will henceforth enter the world of work.

Consciously or not, the whole morning revolves around group bonding. First of all, the University Marshal, the sheriff of Middlesex County, calls the meeting to order. Then a nationally celebrated soprano, later to be made an honorary doctor, sings *America, the Beautiful*, followed by prayers. The Harvard Commencement-Day choir and orchestra sing and play the university hymn *Domine salvum fac*. This forms the introduction, which engulfs all those present in a wave of tradition and patriotism. The atmosphere of solidarity is both visible and tangible.

This is followed by three speeches, the first in Latin and the subsequent two in English, given by the three best students in Latin and English. The themes could best be described as 'traditional': everything is focused on giving thanks to the *alma mater*, underlining the importance of the leadership which all graduates are expected to show in future, and on highlighting the important debt that every Harvard alumnus has to scholarship and society. Eloquent and polished, with remarks about the 'dogs of Yale' – the traditional opponent of Harvard – the only sting in the tail.

The Latin speech is entitled 'Quid durat'[1] ('What will remain?'), and draws a parallel between the passing of the recent long winter and the fact that even Harvard ('quoddam saeculum futurum'; thus, 'in a future world') will one day pass, and may be discovered in ruins in a future century. The central question of the speech is almost rhetorical, and concerns what would then remain of the once so proud Harvard... The correct answer, of course, is that Harvard forges a bond that is more beautiful than any monument of bronze or marble; a bond between alumni, a bond based on the education they received, a bond that is more lasting than any in the world. It is a text that more straight-talking Europeans, especially those in the Netherlands, would find

1   McGlone, J., 2015: *Quid Durat? What Lasts?*, Cambridge, Massachusetts, May 28, 2015.

hard to swallow, but it has a splendid effect, judging by the response of the audience.

And so it goes on; each dean presents each group of graduates as future leaders: business leaders, government leaders, educational leaders, leaders in urban planning and geography. In short, the word 'leader' is the most used and valued word of the morning. Once all of the graduates have received their formal degree certificates, the ceremony concludes with the awarding of ten outstanding honorary doctorates; including, this time, a doctorate for Wally Broecker for his formidable contribution to oceanography.

Before, during and after the morning and afternoon ceremonies, stalls everywhere sell sweatshirts and other paraphernalia in Harvard colours and with Harvard emblems. Groups of alumni take lunch in the separate colleges: old bonds are renewed and re-forged. Together with the just-graduated, the alumni play a central role everywhere, and words such as leadership and responsibility crop up in every possible context. It is a celebration of the 'haves', of the successful, but also, as the president of Harvard emphasizes, of the utilization of opportunities, of hard work, including on the part of students who made it to Harvard from the poorest backgrounds, thanks to help from Harvard scholarships.

The whole afternoon is for the alumni, and now some of the chairs are empty – although there are still 20,000 people walking around campus. The president of the alumni association takes the lead, and she emphasizes everything that the alumni have done for 'their university' in the past year. Medals are presented to the most deserving alumni, including the director/alumnus who brought together Harvard's three great museum collections in one splendidly renovated museum. There are also two speakers for the afternoon programme: Drew Faust and the ex-governor of Massachusetts. To judge from the comments of the onlookers, the latter is a disappointment (previous years' speakers have included J.K. Rowling and Oprah Winfrey), but the former gives, to my mind, a fascinating speech.[2] Without beating about the bush, she attempts to answer the question of how we can justify a classical university such as Harvard, in an era of online learning, of debate about the high costs of education, and of criticism (largely Republican) of the system.

Her argument is surprising in its simplicity. She takes the 'selfie' as her starting point: why has the selfie become so ubiquitous in recent years? Why do people want to photograph themselves in every context and then share this image online? She traces the phenomenon back to the still-dominant 'age of the self', in which people pay more attention to their own experiences, their own achievements and their own rights and duties than those of the community. In her opinion, the individualization that flows from this also lies at the basis of online learning, which can be enjoyed at a time that suits the student, for a fee chosen by the student, and at the cheapest possible price for the highest possible production. More than ever, students are playing the role of consumers. But she rightly signals that this trend has simultaneously made politicians more critical than ever, and particularly critical of the quality and added value of expensive campus education, whereas digital education is suggested to be 'cheaper and better'.

Drew Faust's answer is not entirely satisfactory, but it deserves our attention because she is attempting to answer

2   Faust, D., 2015: http://www.harvard.edu/president/speech/2015/2015-commencement-speech.

a question that we will all face in the coming years. Why should we maintain an expensive campus? Why not teach online, and what is the added value of the university in this day and age? Why all of those costs, if Bill Gates was more than successful as a drop-out? Why does one still need a university in an era when Peter Thiel, a successful Silicon Valley entrepreneur, subsidizes students on condition that they immediately leave college with a good business plan? Drew Faust underlines the major societal role played by the university as one of the world's oldest institutions, in forming students into world leaders, and in teaching the world's young people to take responsibility for others rather than for themselves alone. In turning out citizens of the society of tomorrow instead of self-absorbed individuals. In other words, she does not see 'from knowledge to skill to cash'[3] as the primary justification of the university; she believes above all in the role of the university as the bearer of societal norms and values, in its role as an educator of responsible citizens who will make great contributions to the sustainable society of the future. Only in second place does she emphasize the university's role as the discoverer of the sorely-needed knowledge that will play an essential role in keeping the society of the future running effectively. She is opposed to the notion of an online university, because in her opinion, it is only possible to educate young people, which includes learning to do research, in the context of a community; by living with one another on campus.

At first sight, the events in Harvard on that sunny day in May might lead one to assume that the university as an institution is not at risk, and that after eight hundred

---

3   Slogan used by the Dutch government to promote valorisation and the entrepreneurial university.

years, cracks have yet to appear on the university's bastions. But Drew Faust's argument suggests a different picture: even one of the most prestigious universities in the world has concerns about the future. Listening carefully to her argument, one hears concerns about funding, about social acceptance of the university's role when many in the US are wondering whether the system is not too expensive and whether what students learn is useful, about the rise of the digital university, right up to Peter Thiel's provocative challenge to give university a wide berth and enter the world of work straight away, armed with a good business plan. Clearly, there is also uncertainty about the role that university should play in society in future. Traditions can sometimes help with this, but just as often – and even more often – they are limiting. Admittedly, on a day such as this, everyone basks comfortably in the idea of the traditional campus; but in view of the high costs, isn't a campus actually a huge liability? Answering all these questions demands a constant, keen debate, in which the university must examine its current grounds for existence. A debate in which every stakeholder must participate: students, lecturers and administrators, but also the government and societal actors. Only then will the university be able to prepare for the future.

16. The need for legitimization

In contrast to days gone by, in the coming years universities will have to justify their existence like never before. Until recently, students, lecturers and university administrators were able to assume that the university would play an authoritative and recognized role in society. For many centuries, transferring knowledge was the university's most important task, and the Enlightenment confirmed the university's independence by enshrining the cultural-historical importance of knowledge; that is, knowledge for knowledge's sake. Von Humboldt's ideas placed the university in a far-away ivory tower that for two centuries proved an impregnable fortress – one that was also far from all the hustle and bustle, since the university, in many respects, existed at quite a distance from broader social discourse. And this remained the case until long after the Second World War, when, under pressure from democratization and the mass influx of students that came with this, the university gradually left the ivory tower that had long protected it.

One longstanding and successful form of legitimization was educating young people who would go on to assume leading roles in the state and private sector. From the very first years of its existence, the university guaranteed the quality of its degrees, so that society would be assured of a supply of well-trained graduates. The university supplied the elite – the leaders of the church and the nation – but from the Enlightenment onwards, it did so as an independent institution, thereby avoiding the erosion that has blighted other institutions until now. Over the centuries, the research on which the university increasingly focused also formed an important justification for its existence, because it provided important social benefits, such as those brought by medicine, and later, agriculture and technology.

But it no longer seems possible to take all this for granted. Over the past twenty years, a sometimes heated debate has flared up about the value of the university. This debate has various roots. First, there is the economic background, which mainly became topical as a result of the unprecedented expansion of higher education and the costs that accompanied this, which for many governments were no longer affordable. This means that when assessing how much the government should contribute financially to education, since the 1980s, there have been increasing demands for economic returns: what economic benefits does education bring? What value do graduates bring? Couldn't the same effect be achieved with fewer resources? What is the value of knowledge? These are all questions that measure the university largely in economic terms. In recent years, the maxim of return on investment, which is measured using key performance indicators (KPIs), appears to have won out over the centuries-old public faith that all was well in the ivory tower.

A second threat emerged in parallel to that described above: one that concerned questions about the same independence that the university had maintained for centuries. The incredible growth in digital knowledge exchange via the Internet, among other things, allowed millions of people to gain insight into scientific results, but this went hand in hand with a much greater degree of transparency regarding quality and integrity. It suddenly became clear that scholars were massaging their data, manipulating figures in order to achieve nice results, or sometimes even committing fraud in order to get published in a top journal.

For both of these reasons, the public image of the university was rapidly transformed from that of an ivory tower to that of a massive grey factory, through which large numbers of students were being squeezed as quickly as possible. Society wondered loudly why this should cost so much, whether the university was indeed worth all that investment, given the economic returns, and, moreover, whether scholars were playing fair behind the scenes.

With hindsight, we can see that the university has made a poor job of defending itself in debates about its right to exist. The most common response that one hears is that of the traditionalists, who argue that the university should go back to how it used to be. This group enjoys much support within the university, but carries little authority beyond it. Collini,[1] for example, defends the university mainly from the position of the humanities, making a detailed argument that there are four grounds for justification (supplying an educated workforce; delivering 'useful' knowledge; safeguarding, cultivating and transferring (intellectual) heritage; and contributing to upward social mobility). To give Collini his due, he does correctly identify the tensions that can arise in this regard: 'the self-development of the student' sounds like a wonderful basic task for the university, but everyone knows that there are limits to this, not least from the labour market. He also identifies the danger of 'over-justification', which can occur when defending the university. In her book *Not for profit: why democratization needs the humanities*, for example, Martha Nussbaum almost seems to suggest that respect for and tolerance of others can only develop through a 'great books' course at university.[2] However right the other arguments

1   Collini, S., 2012: *What Are Universities For?*, Penguin Books.
2   Nussbaum, M., 2010: *Not for Profit: Why Democracy Needs the Humanities*, Princeton University Press.

might be, though, and however enthusiastically universities and scholars might use these arguments when it suits them to do so, they cut little ice when it comes to the questions that are being asked in public: they simply fail to address social concerns satisfactorily.

Another response has been that of university administrators, who tend to attempt to legitimize the university on the grounds of its economic value, by increasing support within society for the entrepreneurial university. This is often paired with claims about innovation that are hardly feasible, although it is clear that there is often a relationship between research and innovation, even if this is considerably less direct than universities often suggest.[3]

When reflecting on the university of the future, it appears more important than ever to bear in mind that the basis for its legitimacy can constantly change, given the shifting social dynamics. In different periods and different contexts, and even on different continents and in different countries, the arguments for justification are always slightly different. For this reason, we need a university that is constantly reflecting, constantly debating the question of 'why we are here at all'. In addition to a number of classical basic values that will remain valid, this demands the creation of a set of values that may be subject to rapid change and that should be subject to continuous reflection.

The most classical justification is the historical-cultural one: universities play a pivotal role in the transfer of essential extant knowledge, which is often the conveyor of cultural values and norms. This relates to the very foundations of scholarship and our historical awareness of our existence, as well as the way in which we stand on the shoulders of

3   UNESCO, 2015: 'Science Report, 2015: Towards 2030', www.unesco.org.

our predecessors. The ideas of Galileo and Darwin changed the world so radically that it is only through their work that the world can be understood. This forms a permanent, fundamental basis for the university's existence and one that should constantly be emphasized.

A second legitimization for the university, one that is likewise classical but also entirely valid, is related to education and the way that young people are prepared for roles in society. This objective should be clearly reflected in the nature of the education, which on the one hand should connect to the historical foundations on which our knowledge rests, but on the other hand, should take the form of modern teaching that is tailored to the students' wishes. In view of the latter, this will increasingly mean tailoring education to a changing labour market. As we shall see below, while this means that education should become more demand-driven, the university's abiding task will be to ensure that students receive a thorough training in independent thinking and problem solving.

The third basis that will also make the university indispensable in future – conducting research – is also traditional, but the way in which it is interpreted will change significantly in future. Since the Enlightenment, one fundamental difference between universities and other institutions has been that the former constantly draw links between research and teaching. More than ever, there will continue to be a need for innovative research, but this will bring increasing demand for social benefits. This is at odds with the debate about whether research should be 'free': although traditionalists will argue that research should be funded in full without strings attached, it is inevitable that the economic and above all the social impact of research will have to be made visible, or the whole basis for investment by both public and private financiers will soon disappear. The university, along with the government, should assume specific responsibility for stimulating, safeguarding and protecting innovative and high-stakes research, to avoid the risk of research portfolios becoming too limited as a result of unilateral pressure from societal demand.

The 2008 financial crisis and its aftermath have led to a rapid and profound change in the social climate worldwide. In nearly all Western countries, politicians are going back to focusing on national interests. In this climate, universities are facing a difficult period. Following the election of President Trump in 2016, many[4] anticipate a dark spell in the US, in particular in terms of its leading role in higher education, the excellence of this education, but also – and especially – the role of the US as a place where international students are welcomed. This gloomy picture also applies for the agendas of the European populist parties in countries such as France, the UK, Germany, Italy and the Netherlands: on a general level, the focus on curtailing immigration and the limited attention for higher education that this speaks of are viewed as a threat to the academic community.

In all cases, there is a growing fear of the denial of scientific facts.[5] Here, too, President Trump in the US is setting a prominent example that many are hoping will not be followed by others: the prioritisation of the economy over the environment while at the same time denying the existence of major environmental issues, denying climate

4   Altbach, P.G. & H. de Wit, 2016: 'Will Trump Make US HE Great Again? Not Likely', *Times Higher Education*, November 2016.
5   *Times Higher Education*, 2016: 'Will "Anti-Science" Trump Harm US Research?', November 2016; Jaschik, S., 2016: 'Trump Victory Will Be a Jolt for Higher Education', *Inside Higher Ed*, www.insidehighered.com, 9 November 2016.

change, and his lambasting of the National Institutes of Health as being a waste of funds are not reassuring.

In view of these developments, it is essential that universities clearly establish a position in the societal debate. There will be an increasing need for indisputable facts, and institutions with the authority to provide them. But in order to do this successfully in the 'post-fact' era, universities must be aware of the gap between the higher- and lower-educated. This gap can only be bridged through adequate outreach: not only by stating the facts, but also putting them in context and interpreting them in a broad range of different ways. This includes directly liaising with the media, but also extends to raising awareness and providing information at various different levels, such as through academic hubs and museums or by organising debates. The university must look for ways to successfully approach sections of the population which have long stopped reading the paper or watching television, but which predominantly or exclusively get their information from social media.

The younger generation is essential in this process: Altbach[4] rightly notes that, in the referendums and elections of the past few years, the voting behaviour of students in both Europe and the US is markedly different from that of the older generations. They are predominantly proponents of globalisation, all the more since they are often part of the educated elite and therefore stand to benefit from it. But that also means that students, who in the US mainly voted for Bernie Sanders and therefore against Clinton's establishment and Trump's populism, and in Europe voted against Brexit and in favour of the European Union, will increasingly protest against the populist concept of 'taking care of our own people first'. This places universities in the difficult position of having to straddle conflicting aims: on the one hand, they will have to play a role in bridging the gap in the societal debate with facts and knowledge, but on the other, they will increasingly be populated by young students who will take a clear stance against anti-globalisation and populism. In that sense, universities may once again becomes centres of protest, but at the same time they must avoid being the isolated ivory towers of the elite. Hopefully, universities will be able to help give shape to these protest movements while at the same time strengthening their connection with the 'angry white man'.

In future, the university may well derive its most important form of legitimacy from its visibility and leadership in society. Despite the fact that public discourse is showing less and less interest in complexity, tackling complex problems is one of the university's key strengths.[6] In recent years, the word 'impact' has been used to capture the university's contribution in this respect, a word that partly covers the notion of economic returns. The university can and must play a guiding role – in any case, a visible role – in society, whilst maintaining absolute independence and integrity. The need for such a role has grown strongly due to the eclipse of guiding institutions such as the church, while politics is also becoming less and less ideologically loaded. In the increasingly complex society of the future, in the face of less and less guidance, the university can and must play the role of an intermediary between knowledge and societal problems and phenomena. As explained in previous chapters, open science plays an essential role in this process of developing stronger roots in society, and the university

6   Sexton, J., 2005: *Dogmatism and Complexity: Civil Discourse and the Research University*. Based upon a speech delivered at Katholieke Universiteit Leuven. Unpublished.

must adapt its approach by ensuring an effective flow of knowledge in the direction of society in all kinds of ways.

The greatest task for the university of the future is to be constantly willing and able to adapt all of these potential forms of legitimization, to different degrees and in different forms, to local circumstances and to constantly shifting conditions over time. In times of economic recession, the appeal to make an economic contribution should not be ignored, whereas in times of political crisis, for example, the university could play a major role by contributing to social debate and conducting research into strengthening institutions. We therefore need to see university planning based on portfolios, rather than classical planning based on disciplines. For this is the great challenge: on the one hand, to keep traditional, discipline-based scholarship intact, because it is essential to achieve progress in this, while on the other hand, to allow the results of this scholarship to be used flexibly and often in interdisciplinary ways in social contexts. This means that the university will need to be organized in a flexible, readily adaptable way.

We have now moved very far from the heart of the argument as expressed by John Adams, the second president of the US: 'The whole people must take upon themselves the education of the whole people, and must be willing to bear the expense of it.' That is, education in all of its forms is so important that the responsibility for education and its costs should simply be borne by the state without further discussion. But Adams' statement could also be read in the following way: education is something that is so self-evident that there is no need for any argument or discussion. And this, in fact, is the position taken by quite a number of scholars, including Collini, who believe the value of the university to be so intrinsic that there is no need for any explanation or justification: the university exists and the state should pay for it. But if we follow the example of Adams or Collini – and this is tempting, given its ease and simplicity – then we must realize that in doing so, we will move many miles away from the current debate in society.

Just like every other institution, the university has to justify its existence. It falls to university administrators, in particular, to encourage debate within their institutions. It is often easy for them to draw on significant support when it comes to traditional teaching and research, but society will ask for much more than this in the coming decades, and in many cases less money will be available to pay for it. In addition, we will need to search for new ways to put the university at the heart of society and to adapt its structure to the new context.

17.   Old and new core values

Core values are important for an organization's identity: all being well, they provide a concise and powerful guideline for collective action. They show what an organization *wants* to be, often in contrast to what an organization *is*. Core values capture shared ambitions. Whilst most modern universities do have such values, they often exist on paper alone, certainly not in such an active way that the university community is familiar with them. In future, however, there will probably be a greater need for them than in the past, when universities developed as a matter of course, were very small and faced little criticism from society.

The very first universities did not need any legitimization: they existed thanks to patronage from the church or a sovereign. In terms of its size, the University of Bologna was little larger than the group of legal scholars that, led by Irnerius of Bologna, set about reviving Roman Law. They had an enormous influence, however, on the legal thinking of the budding Renaissance. Nowadays, universities are often institutions with more than 10,000 students and at least around 5,000 employees. Whilst the differences in scale are immense, it is a sobering thought that conversely, the societal impact of the university has declined in proportion to these differences in scale. Over the past decades the debate about the independence, the meaning and even the right to exist of the university has grown. Whilst church and sovereign asked the medieval university to make pronouncements on thorny issues, today the university is blamed for failing to make an adequate contribution to society. An end has come to the golden era of constant growth and unquestioned legitimacy, with the belief that knowledge is an objective in itself that does not have to be justified by immediate economic returns. Although governments are still investing huge amounts in higher education, we appear to be reaching a turning point in thinking about the importance of the university.

Within the university's walls, in particular, this general waning of faith in institutions is not taken very seriously. There is a simple inability to imagine that the time might come when society is able to manage without formal universities. But the history of the newspaper, for example, tells us about the effect that extremely rapid changes in the social context can have. Between 1600 and 1700, newspapers first became a feature of daily life, mainly in Germany and the Netherlands, and later in the century also in France, Scandinavia and England, as a means of spreading news. For many years, the reading of newspapers was limited to the literate and was thus often an elite occupation, but in the twentieth century the newspaper enjoyed its definitive breakthrough as the most influential knowledge-provider of the age. Even the rise of radio did not undermine the ability of the newspaper to take influential, independent viewpoints and thereby play a major social role. Neither did the arrival of television immediately spell the end for the newspaper. Perhaps contrary to expectations, newspapers and television acted as parallel channels of news, and the latter was gathered in comparable ways: particularly in the beginning, the rules of the game of newspaper journalism were copied closely by television reporters.

The death blow for many newspapers was eventually dealt by the rise of new media: computers, the Internet and social media. And with new media, there was also a shift in the tone of the public debate, whereby the wisdom of the crowd, not independence, became the key factor. In this debate, it is no longer essential to know what the truth is. Instead, it is mainly about how many people share the same opinion: it is the power of numbers that counts. After four centuries of newspaper journalism, no one could imagine that interest in both the 'news' and in the very medium itself could falter as rapidly as it has done over the last ten years. No one could have suspected that values such as independence, integrity, correctness and precision would appear to lose their potency so quickly. Yet this has happened, and the impetus was largely given by the unprecedented opportunities offered by new media.

Within the university, the first response has been to seek protection from this rapidly changing context and argue for a return to old values and conditions. Exemplary of this attitude is a much-cited piece in *The Chronicle for Higher Education* by Terry Eagleton,[1] received approvingly by many within the university community and entitled 'The slow death of the university'. The crux of the argument is that the old university is slowly dying as an institution because it has left the ivory tower, and because professors have become managers and students consumers. According to Eagleton, money has become the measure of all things: the university has become an enterprise, even in Oxford and Cambridge, and democratic self-governance led by professors has been replaced by centralized governance by individuals who are increasingly behaving like CEOs. Eagleton renounced his chair in Oxford in protest at these structural changes, but also due to the growing practice of funding scientific and medical disciplines 'at the expense of the humanities', as well as the fact that 'institutions that

1   Eagleton, T., 2015: 'The Slow Death of the University', *The Chronicle of Higher Education*, April 6, 2015.

produced Erasmus and John Milton, Einstein, and Monty Python, [are capitulating] to hard-faced priorities of global capitalism'.

Eagleton makes the case for the restoration of the university as it was fifty years ago, without realizing that this would be impossible. For it is not the university that has changed; rather, it is that the total and utter transformation of society has affected the university. The question is thus not how we might return to the old situation, but what the core values of the new university should be. And the key to this is that whatever choice the university makes in the coming 25 years, it is essential that the balance between independence and interdependence with society should thereby be guarded carefully, and that the reliability of the university should be absolute. In any case, in an age ruled by the wisdom of the crowd, there is an urgent need for one wholly reliable institution. This implies a need for transparency and a willingness to be fully accountable for every piece of data, every conclusion and every opinion. It also means that this should be a top priority within all of the university's processes and agreements.

There are many sides to the core value of independence. One related characteristic is unbridled curiosity, and this is certainly something that the university should maintain. It has traditionally been a characteristic feature of the university, but one that is often limited in the modern context due to funding, for example. Just as for independence, the university should engage in an ongoing attempt to create the conditions for unbounded inquisitiveness, including – and perhaps especially – in its teaching. The university has an important cultural responsibility here, one that is analogous with that of museums, but there is an additional dimension for universities due to the consequences of this knowledge for human action. Here one might think of elements of the humanities such as history, philosophy and ethics – disciplines that are essential for social reflection.

This is reinforced by the fact that nowadays, universities often behave as though government funding and social demand play a determining role in whether disciplines survive: if there is no funding or no demand, then the department or discipline in question is shut down on the grounds of strict financial considerations. Although this is understandable, in future, universities should take more responsibility for ensuring that the range of disciplines is not overly determined from the outside. This is so important that universities might even make use of internal cross-subsidizing – that is to say, using income intended for one discipline to prop up a different field.

Independence and inquisitiveness are longstanding core values that the university of the future will need in full, but these values alone will not be sufficient. More than ever, the university will need a third quality in order to survive and to maintain or regain its authority. Whereas many mourn the fact that the university has left its ivory tower, we should actually take advantage of this in the coming years, in order to become more visible and to play a more significant role in society. This could range from addressing major societal problems to providing knowledge for an informed politics. Rather than withdrawing into its old role, the university should play a leading part in social debate, whilst not for a moment abandoning its independent judgement or the use of correct data. Having a meaningful impact and making meaningful contributions should play key roles when the university makes choices and takes decisions for the future. In this sense, 'impact' is a much better term than 'valorization', which is largely related to the creation of economic ie. Impact goes further, covering all of the contributions that the university can make to social questions and needs, regardless of economic added value.

This brings us, almost automatically, to the fourth and final quality that should be an important feature of the university. Since the Enlightenment, the ideal of knowledge – the gathering of knowledge for knowledge's sake – has come to lie at the very heart of the university. The idea gradually developed that the production of knowledge is always meaningful, even if it results in a huge number of articles that no one reads or cites any more. In the coming years, it is essential that this view evolve into a completely different concept, namely that the university is concerned with something more like wisdom. Analogous to the way in which the university's contribution should be measured in terms of meaningful impact, not in an economic sense, knowledge should be valued to the extent that it functions in the context of a pressing question, and the degree to which it provides a broadly applicable answer.

In a critical intellectual environment such as the university, words such as 'meaningful' and 'wisdom' soon provoke follow-up questions, for behind such terms lie a whole range of potential meanings and implications. Instead of defining these immediately, in the new form of the university, this meaning should be discovered in discussion with the university community and in debate with societal actors. This search is important, because it will allow us to identify precisely which pressing questions we are facing, and how knowledge might contribute to solving these. But it will also be a search to discover when knowledge becomes wisdom; when it becomes a solution or a question that enriches people's lives.

The university of the future will have to work on the basis of these four key qualities, which are largely derived from its old core values: above all on the basis of its independence and inquisitiveness. These core values will automatically lead the university to make a meaningful contribution to society and scholarship. Ideally, scholarship should be about more than knowledge alone, namely about meaningful knowledge or wisdom. Administrators, lecturers and students should continuously steer these values and qualities. The government could also play a role in this, by intervening in the framework at crucial moments, but its role should be limited in order to avoid the whole process being smothered in bureaucratic regulations.

At present, however, we see a very different situation. At a time when funding is falling, universities are steering first and foremost on the basis of their finances, with an eye to balanced budgets and economic returns. In view of this, it is absurd to claim, as Eagleton does, for example, that the university has become a business. University administrators simply have a duty to govern sustainably and create as much stability as possible. Something similar is true of the 'quantity versus quality' debate: whereas quality is undoubtedly essential, society has a right to desire a reasonable return on its investment, in the form of a hardworking university community that delivers many results. What matters here is which principle plays the leading role: the university should be led by a desire to make a meaningful contribution to major issues, whether these are social or scientific. If it is serious in doing so, then these principles should be brought into balance with the available means, and the degree to which economic returns can be demanded. In Northwestern Europe, and particularly in the Netherlands, this is hindered by the fact that the corporate culture of the university is extremely developed, as is the degree to which scholarly production is stimulated. It should come as no surprise that these are often modern, business-like universities that enjoy very high positions in the rankings for scholarly output per employee. But this also means that there will have to be an adjustment in order to achieve the abovementioned balance.

Bureaucratization presents a major problem when it comes to the successful development of the university. There are two sides to this: on the one hand, there is the continuously growing burden of accountability in order to secure funding. On the other hand, there is the increasing burden of accountability for quality, from quality assessments to rankings. The former is harmful because ever-larger sums of money are needed to meet increasing demand from government, among others, for more and more detailed accountability. Trust is the key term here: globally, having a high-trust system would save a great deal of money that could be spent more effectively on teaching and research. This is largely a matter for politicians and not for the university, although the latter should keep arguing for a return to such trust.

But the never-ending spiral of rankings and metrics is a matter for universities themselves. It is clear that despite the extremely dubious basis of the mutual comparisons on which the rankings are based, and the sometimes perverse incentives for increasing scholarly production, governments will continue to need such rankings. After all, rankings offer a clear basis for deciding how to distribute scarce funds. With this in mind, it is inevitable that the bureaucracy that comes with all of this will continue to increase within government, the universities and funding agencies. The universities will have to fight hard against this in the coming decades, because the growing body of league tables has a disruptive effect, putting increasing emphasis on production, impact and fees, rather than quality. They could do so, in particular, by bringing internal metrics back to a minimum. Although this trend is already underway, metrics could be curtailed much more; the more so since it has been shown by the English Research Evaluation Framework, for example, that peer review deviates significantly from metrics and is a better way to assess quality.[2] If the university is unable to free itself from external rankings, which often have a completely irrational basis, then it should at least ensure that a very different climate prevails within the university itself.

In accordance with the above, there should also be radical changes to the system in Europe and elsewhere on a number of points. If reliability is one of the essential core values on which the university's chances of survival depend, then in practice, we should draw as many conclusions as possible in relation to this. This is linked, not least, to the way in which we make core values such as these visible. Key values need to be surrounded by rituals in order to become sustainable.[3] 'Reliability' should thus be made visible in every conceivable way: in today's expensive communication and marketing strategies that tend to sing the praises of the university, in the ways in which students and employees are approached, and in the way in which the university makes financial investments in reliability. Inevitably, faced with unimaginably large quantities of data, universities will have to invest on a truly massive scale in having reliable and useable data files that make knowledge available in an

2   Wooding, S., T.N. van Leeuwen, S. Parks, S. Kapur & J. Grant, 2015: 'UK Doubles Its "World-Leading" Research in Life Sciences and Medicine in Six Years: Testing the Claim?', *PLoS One*. July 2015.

3   Pansters, W.G. & H.J. van Rinsum, 2015: *Enacting Identity and Transition: Public Events and Rituals in the University*, Minerva.

uncontroversial way. Amid a mass of opinions and data, the university will have to stand out as a beacon of reliability as its facilitates society's demand for knowledge, so that knowledge – which is often acquired using public means – is also given back to society. The university must become a trusted oracle once more, instead of being just one of the many opinions, barely audible above the din of the wisdom of the crowd.

But the university will have to do more than this: rewards have a significant effect on behaviour. The university should reward quality, not quantity, and in this sense the promotion and remuneration system should be more focused on quality than is now the case. The fact that this is more easily said than done is shown by the debate about teaching careers that is raging in many countries: whilst it is easy to forge a successful career on the basis of lots of publications in top journals, how difficult it has proven to have a career as an excellent teacher! A totally new HR policy is needed here, one that is separate from the traditional academic systems in which appointments are all too often a form of co-optation. This was the case in the ancient guilds from which many university traditions originate: the masters determined which workers were ready for the big league. Whereas this has the advantage that academic quality is guaranteed in many respects, on the negative side, it leaves little room for change and a remuneration system that is genuinely based on high-quality innovation. Reflecting thoroughly on HR policy will be a core precondition for preserving the vitality of the system.

18. The government and the higher education system of the future

Although the picture is undoubtedly nuanced, virtually everyone believes education to be important for a country's future. On the basis of this widely shared public conviction, governments feel responsible for primary and secondary education. This will certainly remain the case, although we are seeing increasing privatization even in the primary education sector. There is considerably less agreement on the role of government in higher education, though. Although everyone is convinced of its importance, governments take very different positions in relation to the financing and regulation of this sector, decisions that are naturally important for the future of the system. What the government does, whether it is governing at a distance or monitoring the system closely, is decisive: there is no such thing as a government role that has no consequences.

If we compare the continents, the situation in the US can be seen as an extreme where the government is at a great distance from the sector and privatization has advanced significantly. This is less the case in Canada and England, and the distance between the government and higher education then lessens further as one moves from Northern to Southern Europe. The gap is narrowest in Asia, where the government has a strong influence on the future of the system in relation to both funding and regulation. But virtually everywhere else, the coming decades will be defined by further government withdrawal. This is unavoidable, given the predictions of sluggish economic growth, and especially due to the ever-rising cost of providing public healthcare for ageing populations. The government will thus have less and less space to invest in higher education. In the US, there is hardly any leeway for a further shift in this direction: it will be a matter of pulling out the stops to prevent quality standards falling in the present system of public universities, and to prevent the further widening of the divide that currently exists in the system.

In Asia, different choices are likely to be made for the time being: here, the government will have an interest in continuing to play a major role in steering the course of the universities. In particular, investments that lead directly to innovation, economic returns and profits in healthcare will be stimulated. It is thought that economic growth in Asia will continue to be sufficiently high over the coming 25 years to provide space for considerable investment in education. This will undoubtedly put the supremacy of the universities in the US, England and continental Europe under pressure: the quality of Asian universities will certainly rise and with this, there will be a reverse in the brain-drain towards Asia, or at the very least, increased competition for talent.

Although university administrators are constantly asking the government to intervene less, we should reflect in detail on the consequences of the government taking a back seat. That is because the core tasks of the university are implicitly predicated on the existence of three sources of funding. First of all, the state; second, private and industrial partners that pay for knowledge and new technologies; and third, parties that provide funding in exchange for solutions to major social problems. These three forms of financing can be seen as lying at the vertices of a triangle, between which hybrid forms are possible. The Asian universities are located mainly on the side of state funding, with the low level of autonomy that often comes with this, because the state enjoys a significant say in exchange for funding. For certainly in less prosperous countries and developing countries, the state will demand an immediate price for funding in the form of output: universities will have to focus on knowledge that pays. Such pressure edges the system rapidly in the direction of economic returns and links with private capital, and as a result of this, Asian universities will soon be the most entrepreneurial in the world.

Universities in the US are located somewhere on the axis between private and public funding. In the future, they too will increasingly turn to private funding, and they are extremely entrepreneurial. As a result, there is a significant focus on the outside world, but surprisingly enough, there is also a high degree of focus on fundamental research. The latter is not self-evident, given the modest role played by the state, which in many respects is often seen as a guardian of fundamental research, whereas the 'market' often has an interest in instant applications. The English universities are clearly moving in the direction of this model. There, the state will take another step back; at present it is only responsible for research funding. The student, as the user, pays extremely high tuition fees, which will continue to rise. But in England, like the US, a lot of attention is also paid to the public good and societal issues. Just as in the US, this focus on the ideal society can be explained by the fact that the large universities are highly dependent upon donations. From this perspective, a university's image is extremely important, and playing a significant role in society – including in healthcare – is one of the factors determining success in attracting funding.

In continental Europe, universities in the coming decades will also receive funding that is a hybrid of all three components, including significant state intervention. The latter, however, often safeguards a relatively high share of fundamental research. This is closely connected to the political context within the EU, especially in the northern countries, where the state has traditionally upheld relatively strong social-democratic principles when it comes to the distribution of wealth and access to education, compared to the relatively strong liberal or neo-liberal context of the US.

In each country, the nature of funding will have major consequences not only for access to higher education, but also for what the system as whole will be like. We can distinguish roughly two extremes at present, with all possible hybrid forms in between. The system in the US is the most privatized system, with the relatively strict system of selection that often goes with it, whereas in the countries of Northwestern Europe, for instance, we find a system that is dominated by a high level of state funding and free access to higher education, or access for a modest fee. In the US, history has shown there to be a close relationship between higher levels of private financing, selection and differentiation in the system, all of which have significant implications for access to higher education, and is thereby leading to an increasing social divide. Conversely, the more the state is involved in funding and regulation, the more inevitable it becomes that the system shows more homogeneity and less differentiation – as is presently the case in Europe, for example. On the whole, we can expect every system to move further in the direction of the American extreme.

It must be borne in mind in this context that the rise of populist parties will only exacerbate this trend, both in the US and in Europe. After all, these parties argue in favour of a more nationalist approach and protectionism for the existing, domestic market, and, by extension, the restriction of innovation, especially from abroad. There is a strong tendency to stimulate primary and secondary education in particular, in combination with applied knowledge, in order to directly serve domestic markets and interests. Universities receive far less support, as their returns tend to become visible only in the longer term, and are dependent on the sort of global cooperation which runs directly counter to more nationalist views.

This reduction in the focus on higher education goes hand in hand with the promotion of for-profit education. President Trump has already indicated that he sees this to be an important growth market, which makes it possible to provide high-quality education relatively cheaply, with significantly lower overheads than those of the established institutions. This sentiment chimes with a strong movement – once again, mainly in the US – which feels that universities deliver too little at too high a cost, and, in particular, waste resources on excessive expenditure on campuses and bureaucracy. These critics describe higher education as 'too costly, with too little learning, being intolerant or contemptuous of free expression and diversity of opinion, and producing students who are increasingly underemployed'.[1]

We can explore what exactly further withdrawal on the part of the government would mean with reference to the Dutch system. The system in the Netherlands is currently one in which access to higher education costs relatively little. The academic year begins with a large influx of students who are starting new programmes of study after gaining their secondary school diplomas. There is no additional selection at this point, because the state demands maximum access and having

1   Vedder, R., 2016: 'Mr. Trump: 12 Ways to Reform Higher Education', *Forbes*, http://www.forbes.com/sites/ccap/2016/12/20/mr-trump-12-ways-to-reform-higher-education/#9087ba479a00.

successfully completed pre-university education is seen as a sufficient guarantee of quality. With the continuous flood of new students, it will prove impossible to sustain this position in the near future, due to the mass nature of higher education and the need to curb costs. The government will therefore be compelled to choose between significantly increasing tuition fees, as happened in England, or using selection to limit access to only the most talented students; or both. One should also bear in mind that despite the lack of selection, the Netherlands has proved capable of constructing an excellent system of higher education. All of its universities are in the world's top 200, and there is an unprecedentedly high level of scholarly production compared with other countries, and a lot of attention is paid to the quality of teaching on average; and all this at a reasonable cost.[2,3] But the limits of the system's ability to keep running effectively, given diminishing resources and a large influx, now appear to have been reached.

The consequence of having such a high proportion of state funding is that the Dutch system and similar systems are usually homogenous and 'flat'; there is little difference either between the best and worst universities, or between the different types of university. The government's demands ensure a level playing field in terms of quality, where the differences are small in every respect. If the government takes a step back, as happened in the US, this will irrefutably lead to a higher education system with more differentiation between public and private universities, with absolute peaks in a system that is in fact, on average, relatively mediocre. In this system, the increase in tuition fees in particular,

2   *Times Higher Education*, 2016: 'Europe's 200 Best Universities: Who Is at the Top in 2016?', March 2016, 36-47.

3   OESO, 2015: *Education at a Glance 2015: OECD Indicators*, OECD Publishing, Paris. DOI: http://dx.doi.org/10.1787/eag-2015-en.

together with selection, will lead to greater competition and especially to an ongoing stimulus to improve the quality of teaching and research. After all, the public will only be willing to keep paying high fees if universities with good reputations deliver high-quality education, meaning that the costs borne by the student can be earned back once they have completed their degrees.

For Europe and the Netherlands, the key question in the coming years will be how, given increasing privatization, the major problems that now characterize the public part of the American system in particular could be avoided. As suggested above, the history of America shows that the government's contribution should not fall below a critical limit. Up to a level of around 30%, the withdrawal of government funding can be compensated relatively easily with increased tuition fees; in other words, by having the student pay for the financial contraction. In countries such as the Netherlands, the introduction of higher tuition fees will probably also be defended in public debates and in politics with the idea that this may lead to better motivation among students; the intuitive notion is that countries with low tuition fees have high drop-out rates, because students have relatively low levels of motivation. After all, the game entails no great personal risk that would lead to greater commitment. Nevertheless, this idea is not supported by the data on average drop-out rates in OECD countries.[4] Recent data from England, however, do show an effect since dramatic increases in tuition fees were introduced there.[5]

4   OESO, 2009: 'How Many Students Drop Out of Tertiary Education?', *Highlights from Education at a Glance 2008*, OECD Publishing.
5   Bradley, S. & G. Migali, 2016: 'The Effect of a Tuition Fee Reform on the Risk of Drop Out from University in the UK'. *Economics Working Paper Series* 2015/16, Lancaster University.

In recent years, governments around the world have had less of a tendency to privatize research than teaching. Or to put it the other way around: at the national level, governments have always reserved relatively large sums of money for research. Practically throughout the world, such funding is made available on a competitive basis via national research foundations such as the Natural Environment Research Council (NERC) in the UK, the Netherlands Organization for Scientific Research (NWO) and the National Science Foundation (NSF) in the US. The idea behind this is that research can be used to defend national interests that are less easy to privatize than education, where students provide the replacement funding. Over the last ten years, however, national research funding globally has suffered cuts, and this will certainly continue. That is to say that here, too, the government will have to make choices in the coming decades and will often do so on a sectoral basis, thereby giving more money to areas that are considered more important. This trend is already evident in the Netherlands due to the diminished share for the arts and humanities in comparison with the natural, medical and technical sciences, as a result of the so-called top sectors policy.

In addition to this contraction in competitively-awarded research funding, we can also expect a trend towards providing the structural research resources received by universities on a more 'dynamic' basis; that is to say, more competitively. One example of this approach is England, where the element of competition and differentiation between the universities is heightened by making 80% of the total amount of funding available to 20% of universities. The Research Evaluation Framework was set up in order to regulate this, whereby a university's ranking is determined using peer review for each individual sector and as a whole. In England this development was combined with a sharp rise in tuition fees to cover the costs of teaching. Thus to a large degree, this part of the university has already been privatized.

In Northwestern European countries in particular, such as the Netherlands and Denmark, there is probably a fairly high degree of willingness to create a similarly competitive and differentiated system, because on the one hand, this would respond to the demand for increased university funding through a rise in tuition fees, and on the other hand, greater differentiation would produce a system that would be more competitive vis-à-vis England, for example. In countries such as Germany, and possibly also Sweden, where education has traditionally been virtually free and widely accessible, such a change will remain politically and socially impossible for many years. The same seems true of the Southern European countries where universities have traditionally provided something that is closer to professional training, and the cost of access is relatively low. In such countries, where government funding and broad access will continue to prevail, the system will continue to be the least differentiated and the chances of more autonomous and competitive universities emerging in the coming decade will be relatively low.

Funding will form the key axis along which the differentiation of universities will further develop. In addition to (partly) publicly financed universities, the share of for-profit higher education will develop at a rapid pace. Given that this is market-driven, these institutions will initially develop as niche universities, such as those specializing in business administration, law and economics. In addition, however, there is a lot of room in the more professionally-oriented parts of the education sector, such as healthcare, certainly when teaching is kept relatively separate from the frontline of research. The more that teaching lends itself to digital learning, the more differentiation there will be; and it is here that for-profit universities will have the greatest chance of developing a significant market share.

In view of the massive implications of the shift from public to private funding, the government will *have* to play a role in the system. This is not only the case for teaching, but also for research. Although government intervention is seldom appreciated by university administrators, the interests at stake are simply too great not to hold an intensive debate about the direction in which a country wants to, or should, go. After all, less government intervention almost automatically implies a more private, and thus more selective, system, which will simultaneously become more differentiated because it is more market-driven. This will be paired with a rise in social inequality, which can have serious effects in the long term. By contrast, maintaining a widely accessible system requires having an active, committed government that remains willing to invest in higher education. However, this is often paired with regulations that apply equally to all, thereby hindering differentiation. Ideally, governments and universities would be able to agree upon how to establish widely accessible and yet highly differentiated systems in the coming decades, in order to create a flexible and accessible knowledge economy.

19. The global university and the knowledge ecosystem of the future

'Internationalization' is currently a buzzword in every university, regardless of where it is in the world. In the coming decades, too, there will be increasing collaboration between universities at the global level, whereby the academic global village seems to be becoming a reality. But is this really the case? It is clear that talent will find it easier than ever to search for the best opportunities worldwide, and global student exchanges offer possibilities, but will the role of universities change fundamentally with this, or will they always play important national and even regional roles?

John Sexton[1] has described the importance of the period between 800 and 200 BC as an era in which in a whole series of cultures, fundamental questions were asked by all of the great philosophers: from Confucius in China, the followers of Zoroaster in Persia, the great prophets of the Levant, to the Greek philosophers such as Pythagoras, Plato and Aristotle. Following the German philosopher Karl Jaspers, some describe this period as the 'first Axial Age'. Sexton suggests that the new millennium marked the beginning of a second Axial Age in world history, one characterized by total globalization. He argues that a global civil society is emerging that will lead, in stages, all cultures to come together and interact. In this context, Sexton aptly cites the Greek philosopher Diogenes of Sinope, who, when asked

1   Sexton, J., 2010: *Global Network University Reflection*. Unpublished address. December 21, 2010.

where he was from, is said to have answered: 'I am a citizen of the world'; a cosmopolitan.

The naivety of this belief in unlimited globalization is revealed by a UNESCO study entitled 'Towards 2030'.[2] On the one hand, the study clearly shows that there is increasing international mobility within academia, and moreover, that scholarship is taking place within a truly global network. On the other hand, a more important observation is that this increasing globalization is being influenced more than ever by geopolitical events, such as the relations between the major economic blocks, but also, for example, those in the Middle East. In the coming decades, Southeast Asia will become a formidable knowledge region as well as an economic block, which will no longer function as a point of departure for people, but will attract them. A knowledge region is also emerging in Africa, one that will develop separately from the EU and Asia. It appears that exchange with Russia, including scholarly exchange, will remain limited for some time. Globalization is thus occurring, but at the same time, we are seeing the formation of major knowledge blocks in which mobility and the exchange of knowledge appear to be becoming more autonomous.

Globalization and internationalization will nevertheless form powerful motivations for the changes that universities will experience in the coming 25 years. There is an urgent need to keep up with the global developments and thereby retain access to talent and innovation. But all too often, there is a tendency to think first in terms of student mobility. Although this is very important, attracting top lecturers and researchers is at least as important. Besides staff and student mobility, in the long-term, possibly the

2   UNESCO, 2015: '*Science Report, 2015: Towards 2030*', www.unesco.org.

most important phenomenon will be the growing distinction between universities that operate at the local, regional, national or supranational levels, or even at a truly global level. This last category of universities will attract the top talent, not least because this is where the major funding flows will circulate.

Funding flows will also determine the sites of very large facilities that will play a decisive role in the natural, medical and technological sciences, for example. In this respect, Asia – followed by the US, and Europe at a distance – will almost certainly take the lead. In order to retain a prominent position nevertheless, it is essential that countries that are struggling to finance increasingly expensive equipment can agree on partnerships and national roadmaps that promote coordination. This is already the case in most European countries, but not only national, but also supranational coordination is rapidly becoming necessary, given the huge rise in the level of financial investment that is needed for increasingly expensive equipment.

The rankings, for example, are already revealing the degree to which international collaboration can play a decisive role in a university's visibility and position. European and Asian scholarly production is often rated highly, but ratings for reputation, internationalization and the proportion of international staff and students are considerably lower. This lost ground is often attributed to language: traditionally, Anglo-Saxon countries have simply had the advantage of being English-speaking. The relatively closed culture of European countries, for example, which are less open to foreigners, can also play in role in this, however. Over time, this may prove a threat to their position among the top research nations, which are still dominated by Anglo-Saxon countries on the basis of language and tradition. In the coming 25 years, being able to offer a real international classroom will be one of the decisive factors that counts at the international level.

If universities wish to remain at the top, it will be essential to have access to the global reservoir of talent. And this will mean having a truly cosmopolitan gravitational pull, or at least a good network in which talent circulates. In the US, a number of universities have invested considerable sums, in different ways, in expanding their access to this international pool of knowledge and talent. New York University has gone the furthest in this respect by opening three international portal campuses, together with a large number of study-away sites. Universities such as Yale and Duke have also opened international campuses. Since the trend took off at the start of the millennium, however, it has become clear that this is an expensive and not universally profitable form of globalization. Profitable, in this sense, refers not so much to money, as it is clear that such approaches cost a great deal of money, but also to the intellectual benefits, which are not always great. After a period of expansion and commitment to opening multiple international campuses, British universities have also taken a step back from this approach.

For the American universities, it is critically important to internationalize, all the more so given that the number of international students in the US is already lower than in the EU. We can thus expect North American universities to remain active in this respect through mergers, stakeholding and opening campuses, first in Asia, and second in the Middle East. In view of geopolitical developments, however, this latter region will continue to be risky in the coming years, and China in particular is distancing itself more and more from foreign universities that ultimately attract more Chinese talent than they collaborate with Chinese institutions.

Internationalization is also crucial for Europe, of course, but here, efforts to establish branch campuses have been on a much more modest scale than in America. In view of the financial risks, the emphasis, in addition to maintaining a limited presence in Asia, will lie primarily on boosting student mobility and attracting students from outside the EU. In addition, the EU will invest considerable sums in improving collaboration between universities within the EU, and in particular in stimulating a better distribution of excellent institutions between Eastern and Western Europe: much will undoubtedly be invested in programmes such as the 'Stairway to Excellence' in the coming years.

The picture in Asia completes that in America and Europe: there will be a lesser degree of acceptance of the establishment of branch campuses, particularly in China. This has much to do with the strengthening of national institutions, but also with governmental politics, which views academic freedom as problematic. We can also expect that sooner or later, problems of freedom of expression and academic freedom will become major issues in China and in other parts of Asia and the Middle East. This will eventually become a decisive factor inhibiting the development of further branches in these countries. We can expect partnerships to be encouraged, however, especially with illustrious institutions in the US and Europe. As suggested above, the flow of talent will slowly turn in the direction of Asia. This will pose a threat first to the US, and then to Europe, in the form of the loss of talent.

The least risky form of globalization in future will take place via networks of collaborating universities, such as the League of European Research Universities (LERU), for example, or the European University Association (EUA). There are increasing numbers of formalized networks such as these, and their impact is also becoming more and more visible. In this respect, LERU is an example of a network that has been successful politically in the past decade and has acquired much influence within the EU. What such networks often lack, but will increasingly gain, is substantive partnership and structural mobility. The European Research Area is the key to this in Europe, and in future, the creation of a global research area could also guarantee open borders for scholarship at a global level. LERU has a number of rapidly growing platforms for disciplinary cooperation, in which expertise is also shared. It is a matter of time before structural mobility also gets going, particularly in relation to students, but possibly also to staff in future. In this sense, collaborating within networks could be Europe's answer to opening of branch campuses or holding stakes in other universities, as the mainly privately-financed universities in America and England have done. The network university appears to be becoming the model for the coming decade. One variant of this is the 'triangle university': a triangle of collaborating universities on three continents that aim to profit optimally from various developments.

As we saw at the beginning of this chapter, in the coming decades, the university will increasingly find itself split between two levels, best summarized as 'think globally, act locally'. Globalization will largely entail the exchange of knowledge and, even more so, of talent. The universities that are most active at the global level will shape the academic landscape and the international agenda. At the same time, the regional knowledge system is becoming more and more important. Every university will become increasingly dependent for its development on urban areas that combine a concentration of talent with significant opportunities for innovation. At present, all of the world's top universities form part of a global knowledge hub that is embedded in the context of large urbanized areas, and this will certainly also be the case in future. In the coming decades, urbanization in Asia alone will result in a hundred or so mega-cities: although not every one of these will have the same prospects for developing into a global knowledge hub, it is clear that there will consequently be a significant shift in the direction of Asia.

Over the next few years, the internationalisation of the universities in the Western world may be affected by the growing political trend towards nationalism and populism. These changes are exemplified by the statements of politicians in Europe and the US who are advocating nationalist political agendas with closed borders and severely limited immigration. But in a lot of cases, it goes further than this, with their statements having all the hallmarks of 'taking care of our own people first': the labour market must be protected against foreign workers. In addition to economic motives, these views are often coloured by other sentiments, related to ethnicity and a certain nostalgia for the past and the comparative safety of relative isolationism, of being 'among one's own kind'.

The most immediate effects of isolationist politics can already be seen in the decline in the number of foreign students at universities in Australia, but also in Europe and the US. The election of President Trump and Brexit are sure to contribute to a further reduction in international exchange in the academic world in the US and the UK, respectively. For universities, some of which derive more than 30% of their income from foreign students, this could have a massive impact – especially for the top universities, which

ently have the largest share of students from Asia, for example. In 2014–2015, the 1,000,000 foreign students in the US and the 312,000 foreign students in the UK jointly paid billions of euros' worth of tuition. The fact that foreign students are 'big business' is further evidenced by the fact that Australian universities annually invest 250 million AUD in the recruitment of foreign students alone.[3] But the impact will not only be financial: a large proportion of the talented young minds that flock to these universities every year, especially in the US, come from abroad. A reduction in this influx is sure to affect the quality of these institutions in the decades to come.

In Europe in the coming decades, there will also be considerable momentum towards further regionalization, including under the influence of EU policy. In addition to London, for example, which will certainly obtain its place as a global knowledge-hub, powerful regional knowledge systems will emerge in Southern Germany and possibly Scandinavia, and there will certainly be opportunities for the Dutch Randstad to join them. Reports by the WRR and the Dutch Advisory Council for Science, Technology and Innovation (Adviesraad voor wetenschap, technologie en innovatie, AWTI) rightly point to the importance of regionalization and regional clusters in the knowledge eco-system, but they may be viewing these on too small a scale. On this smaller scale, in any case, there will be significant opportunities in the west of the Netherlands, possibly in connection with Amsterdam, and in the centre of the Netherlands, in connection with the southern Netherlands (the Brainport initiative).

3   Besser, L., P. Cronau & H. Cohen, 2015: 'Universities Embroiled in Foreign Student "Feeding Frenzy" Driven by Corrupt Middlemen', *ABC News*, 17 April 2015.

Universities need to cooperate more in order to create truly regional knowledge-hubs, and the government should give much more encouragement to this mutual collaboration. The rule of thumb here seems to be that clustering what are in principle mutually competitive institutions of equivalent value is often doomed to fail, although there are indications that this will increasingly happen in future. Despite this, the approach can be useful, because equivalent institutions can also build up powerful networks that have a regional impact and are more visible at the global level. One example of such collaboration is that between Strasbourg, Colmar, Basel and Karlsruhe, of which only the last is a technical university, whilst the first three are broad general universities. In addition, we will see a great increase in forms of cooperation or clustering in the coming decades, and these may well be more successful: cooperation between groups of universities that differ from one another, such as a research university with teaching universities and digital universities. Clusters of completely unlike knowledge institutions (universities with colleges of professional and vocational education) may also have potential, however, as the example of Arizona State University shows.

It is not inconceivable that in a number of cases, we will also see demand for more national-level collaboration within smaller countries such as Denmark, the Netherlands and Switzerland, and within larger regions, such as Scotland or the German federal states. The American state system, such as the California or Ohio university system, can serve as an example for this. In this, a flagship can profit from the whole network, whilst the network benefits from the top position of the flagship university. Although the system brings advantages, its preservation requires active state involvement, and we cannot expect to see the rapid emergence of a similar top-down collaborative structure in the Netherlands, for example, or other countries. In this sense, Denmark offers the most recent European example of a partnership at the national level that has been compelled by the state, in which the first cracks are now becoming visible. The American state systems also appear to have had their day: the individual universities want to raise their own profiles rather than get lost in the whole system, leaving all the glory to a single top university.[4]

4   *Times Higher Education*, 2016: 'The California Dream Is Still Golden'. March 2016, 34-37.

20. How will the comprehensive research university survive?

The university in its classical form will undoubtedly change rapidly into a flexible organization that creates and transfers a great deal of digital knowledge. What is more, *the* university will cease to exist: a greater diversity of specialized universities will emerge, varying from the teaching university to smaller niche universities that specialize in agriculture, technology or medicine. The comprehensive research university will encounter difficulties in this respect precisely because of its breadth, to which much importance has traditionally been attached. Breadth offers many opportunities for innovation and combining research, and it is also attractive for students, due to the wide range of teaching options from which they can choose. But at the same time, it is an almost impossible to excel across a whole range of disciplines and to compete with smaller, more specialized universities. Combining teaching and research over this whole range of fields will also constitute a major challenge, even though this was what lay at the core of Van Humboldt's message: namely, the ongoing training of young people in innovative research during their university education.

The coming years will see a revolution in the availability and transfer of knowledge. Whereas for many centuries the university had primacy over knowledge in the form of lecturers and books, knowledge is now a widely-available public good, and publishing companies are even striving to provide and digitally support components of entire curricula. Academia has lost its exclusive rights for good, and this trend will only become stronger in the coming years. First of all, this will have implications for forms of teaching. In the coming 25 years, we will see a strengthening of all kinds of digital learning forms, in the form of MOOCs and SPOCs, but also in various kinds of blended learning. Regardless of the form of learning, demand will become more and more centralized (problem-based learning), at the expense of the disciplinary fundamentals. There will also be a sharp rise in the modularization of teaching in order to accommodate the wishes of students, who will no longer demand whole curricula, but multiple modules tailored to their needs and tastes. In short, there will be a significant shift in the direction of tailor-made and customized learning.

The trends in IT and their consequences will result in a sharp distinction between a number of types of universities. The main distinction will be between research and teaching universities. Research will form a relatively small share of the latter category, and the teaching will largely take place at the level of foundational education; what is now the Bachelor's programme. Within this, there will be a further division into niche universities and broad teaching universities. The former category will see the emergence of a whole series of small, largely digital institutions that offer specialized Bachelor's programmes. We can already see the first signs of this, especially in MBA and law programmes, but other disciplines will be added. There will be a significant increase in these institutions in countries with more liberalized education regulations, and a sharp increase is visible in the US. But the greatest growth in the coming years can be expected in Asia, where demand for university education is so great that there will be a significant need for these institutions, which charge relatively low tuition fees.

Another factor playing a role here is that supervision and quality control in Asia are still relatively mediocre, leaving a great deal of space for this development.

Europe will see much more modest growth in digital niche universities, all the less so where there is already an accessible, relatively cheap and high-quality university system. The Netherlands, Scandinavia and Switzerland may well be growth-countries for this kind of niche university, but not to the extent that this could happen in Asia. This may be an advantage in the short term, but could also lead insidiously to their falling behind in the long term.

In addition to these niche universities, teaching universities will increasingly be recognized as such, including in Europe and Asia, where most universities have traditionally aimed to be broad research universities and have thus nurtured teaching and research to an equal extent. Whereas there is already a relatively broad system of teaching universities in the US, in the form of the colleges, in recent years this has also increasingly been the case in England. As a result of the government's policy of allocating 80% of research funding to the top 20% of universities, the system has in effect been sliced in two; teaching universities are emerging that will probably also do some research, but only a modest amount. This division will also emerge elsewhere in Europe, because there will be increasing financial scarcity, and consequently increasing competition for dwindling amounts of research funding.

Broad teaching universities may well provide much of their teaching digitally, but they will nevertheless try to capitalize on the educational advantages of having a physical location – a campus – for students, and to use this as a weapon in the battle against the digital university. Due to the high tuition fees that will also be needed to offset the high costs of maintaining a campus, however, the broad digital university will nevertheless gain ground, especially in America, and will undermine the system of what are often publicly-financed teaching universities or colleges. When the government takes a further step back, all of the costs, including campus costs, will be passed onto the user, the student. This suggests that the more the government participates in the system and acknowledges the importance of good education, the more likely there is to be room for the campus-based teaching university. This will certainly remain the case in Northwestern Europe in the coming years, where there is even room for the growth of residential Liberal Arts and Sciences (LAS) colleges, for example, although this growth will be limited in view of the higher costs of residential education and the competitiveness of other forms of education. In addition, there is a great future for the campus-based teaching university in Asia: much value has traditionally been attached to physical, face-to-face education in Asia, and lecturers are still held in great esteem. Good colleges, residential or otherwise, are thus in high demand, and students are willing to pay high tuition fees in order to attend an illustrious institution.

In future, another distinguishing characteristic of the research university versus the (digital) teaching university will be the constant linking of teaching and research. This means that the more research plays a visible role in a research university, even in the undergraduate phase, but especially, of course, in the graduate phase, the stronger the university's *raison d'être* will be. In a number of countries, there is a tendency to separate out universities and research institutes; Germany and France are two such examples. One also finds such institutions in the Netherlands – such as those of the Royal Netherlands Academy of Arts and

Sciences – which, as in Germany, France and other countries, date from the beginning of the twentieth century, when the expansion of research mainly occurred via academies of science and governmental funding agencies such as the Dutch NWO.

There will be a trend towards bringing these institutes together in clusters of collaborative institutions in which universities also play a role. In recent decades, moves have already been made in many countries to link such institutions to universities, in any case, or to establish them on university campuses in order to create more added value. Independent, often small institutes such as these are struggling both financially and academically, and they need at least one affiliation with another institution in order to survive. This trend appears to be irreversible, not least because a number of analyses have shown that linking teaching and research is not only relatively cheap,[1] but also beneficial in terms of scholarly production and the quality of teaching in the Master's phase. Only exceptionally powerful organizations, such as the Max Planck institutes in Germany, may be able to keep functioning independently in future, largely thanks to the enormous amount of state funding they receive, but even in this case, only if they collaborate with universities, for example.

In future, students will frequently enter the labour market having completed part of or a whole Bachelor's degree, whereas only a very small proportion of students, ones who are actually interested in research and suited to it, will attempt to obtain a PhD. It currently seems that the doctorate will also retain its value over the coming 25 years, as there

---

1   Ministerie van Financiën, 2014: *Interdepartementaal Beleidsonderzoek Wetenschappelijk onderzoek.*

is a great deal of demand in this top segment of the labour market. A significant share of research will continue to be done in the doctoral phase, and in future this will also be the most productive part of the university when it comes to innovative research and publications. The status and quality of the Graduate Schools that are increasingly hosting this second phase, following the American model, will thereby play a decisive role in the research university's chances of survival. This means that the US – certainly with regard to the private Ivy League institutions – is enjoying a major head start; these institutions already offer a very strong graduate phase with stringent selection of the very best students, plus the presence of sufficient financial resources. In Asia there is likewise recognition of the importance of top research universities, and here, too, the government has sufficient financial leeway to invest: any ground that has been lost will quickly be made up, and within ten years, the top hundred universities will include a considerable number of Asian institutions.

Viewed from this perspective, Europe faces a problem in the coming years: although there is a broad system of universities, the doctoral phase often lacks a sufficiently distinct profile, plus there will be limited financial means in future. Much ground could be lost as a result, certainly if sufficient attention is not paid to both funding and the development of a strong system of graduate schools, in which top research is combined with the very best talent. On the other hand, doctoral students do enjoy excellent training in Europe: Swiss, English and Dutch doctoral programmes, for example, are characterized by creativity, independence and quality, partly on the basis of thorough preparation and training, and these characteristics should be strengthened in the coming years in order to be able to meet the competition coming from the US and Asia.

Compared with other forms of education, the research university is vulnerable in the sense that top-level research is extremely capital-intensive. More than is currently the case, in future top universities will be characterized by advanced technical facilities, which in turn will attract top researchers. This will be the case not only for the natural, medical and technological sciences, but also, increasingly, for the arts and humanities. The best-resourced universities will enjoy an immediate advantage here, but even they will be forced to make fundamental choices due to the enormous rise in the cost of facilities in the coming years. In an attempt to make up the lost ground that will emerge in relation to the massive investments that Asian and some American universities will be able to make, some of the best European universities will probably make choices when it comes to research, and will thereby erode the comprehensive nature of their universities. This will allow them to make smart investments in some research areas, but naturally this will come at a cost to other parts of the spectrum, where the university will have to allow other institutions to occupy the top positions.

Universities could also chart an alternative course by working with other institutions so that they nevertheless achieve expensive facilities such as these, and thereby maintain their top positions, for instance on a regional scale. One excellent example of this approach in Europe is CERN, where numerous countries and scientists collaborate in the area of fundamental physics. Choices can also be made at the national level: a government could invest money in a concentrated way in top facilities that would develop a national character, that is to say, that would be accessible to other universities, too. Examples of this include the Dutch infrastructure road map and its European counterpart.

Finally, we will increasingly see another key strategy in future, one of collaboration between universities and businesses, within or beyond science parks. This will often entail the sharing of equipment, and will sometimes take the form of open innovation, whereby businesses pay to use parts of university laboratories and equipment, or they jointly pay and share. It is clear that universities will try to use a mix of all these strategies: regional collaboration in science parks and beyond in order to optimize their facilities profile, whether or not this entails making difficult choices within their own research.

Most universities will also have to make radical choices on another front. As a consequence of the enormous increase in the amount of data and their use, in the coming years research IT and big data will be ubiquitous, and this will unquestionably transform the nature of scholarship. One important element of this change will be that it will be possible – and rewarding – to combine different sets of data more broadly. In itself, this will reinforce the tendency towards more interdisciplinary research. The latter will also be strengthened by the second change: if universities become more open to societal issues, then this will almost automatically mean that research will be driven more by these issues, with the consequence that in almost every case, the degree of multi-disciplinarity or interdisciplinarity will increase. We can still expect to see large shifts here, completely in line with the great convergences that are, in part, already occurring.[2]

---

2   National Research Council, 2015: *Facilitating Interdisciplinary Research*, The National Academies Press. See also: Wernli, D. & F. Darbellay, 2016: 'Interdisciplinarity and the 21st Century Research-Intensive University'. LERU position paper 2016.

It is certainly not inconceivable that research, in many respects, will become independent of a particular discipline or place, whereby researchers meet in digital space and share their results in the cloud. The first part assumes the formation of increasingly fluid and research consortia, especially digital ones, allowing data to be produced in all kinds of places, on the grounds that digital data can be shared and processed effortlessly. This probably means that there will have to be a radical change in the way that universities are organized in the coming years. Much more than there being permanent structures in the form of departments or groups, such as those that have traditionally been based on the nature of the research, there will be project organizations (which may or may not be based in departments or faculties) that can design interdisciplinary research and education in the context of temporary working relations and in a flexible way.

Whilst it is essential to focus on interdisciplinarity, the great challenge will be to avoid neglecting disciplinarity and disciplinary progress; careful steering will be needed to preserve the balance between the two. This will be difficult if research becomes largely demand-driven: if this happens, the disciplinary track could lose too much of its protection. The state, or the university, should pay particular attention to this and reserve funding specifically for this purpose. The issue goes deeper, however: it is only in the surroundings of a comprehensive research university – that is, a broad research university – that all kinds of new combinations of scholarship, and all kinds of new interdisciplinary forms of research, are able to emerge and flourish. This alone makes the case for careful decision-making and the maintenance of a broad range of disciplines for as long as possible.

A further shift by the university towards the social arena, such as that which will be necessary in the coming years, will also require a different structure elsewhere in the university. In order to design this part of the mission, libraries and university museums will have to change from being internal service-providing organizations into being external figureheads. A university needs antennae in society, but conversely, society largely sees the university through the library, the museum and other forms of outreach. As noted above, the case for lifelong learning implies exactly this context, especially for alumni, but also for others. In this way, the university participates more deeply in societal processes, whereby one should not forget that the 'unbundling' of courses and leaving university early will become more common in future. Alumni and others will then be able to continue learning in a problem-based fashion, based on the questions that arise in the context of their job or role in society.

The process of setting the global scholarly agenda will slowly change in the coming years. In addition to science and technology as paths to greater prosperity, issues that are demanding our attention – such as environmental crises, the food situation and energy issues – will increasingly come onto the agenda.[3] Most universities will undoubtedly adapt their academic portfolios by focusing on the cutting edge of major scientific and societal questions. This will give them a visible and valuable share in the societal debate, leading to their becoming more deeply rooted in society. For this is an important element: students will also assess and select universities on the basis of the contribution they make to society. The research university will also have to play a more significant role in the world's future, whether this is by producing graduates in the form of responsible

3   UNESCO, 2015: 'Science Report, 2015: Towards 2030', www.unesco.org.

citizens who contribute to the society of tomorrow, or by providing lifelong learning after leaving university, or by solving major social and scientific problems.

In addition to the greater focus on major societal issues, the research university of the future will also pay more careful attention to labour market demand. We can expect that professionals with a broad education, as well as disciplinary specialists, will be in demand. There have always been examples of these; think of the natural scientists who pursue successful careers in banking or computer science. But the need for such people will increase the more that knowledge becomes more easily available via large knowledge systems, and as the emphasis shifts from the development of knowledge to the use of generated knowledge.

21. The curriculum of the future

Viewed traditionally, it is the mission of the university to train young people. Providing a highly trained labour force in the form of a social elite has always been something that the university has done successfully. From its founding until deep into the seventeenth century, for instance, the University of Salamanca was almost exclusively responsible for producing all of the key officials and administrators needed to serve the growing Kingdom of Spain and the Habsburg Empire. But all that is in the past; the question is, what kind of graduate will be needed in the future?

In Western European universities in particular, education has become more and more specialized in recent decades, and university training is dominated by the acquisition of what is largely disciplinary knowledge. The balance has often tipped in favour of the latter at the cost of the former. By contrast, the first phase of academic training in American universities is broad, but there, too, we see an increasing shift away from the provision of a broad college education, and a growing number of voices in favour of using the university in a more targeted fashion as preparation for the labour market, also in view of the costs. What is certain, however, is that the labour market that we normally take for granted, which has been employing graduates for centuries, is undergoing a fundamental transformation. A factor that is also playing a major role in this, of course, is the sharp rise in the supply of graduates. Whereas for many years, employment could almost be taken for granted, nowadays we see a general contraction of the labour market and considerable competition, whereby only the very best have a high chance of success. In such a situation, the extent to which a university programme is tailored to rapidly changing demand from society is becoming increasingly important.

We should not be surprised by the fact that too little attention is often paid to the labour market, when we bear in mind that university curricula tend to be supply-driven, that is, driven by academic traditions or lecturers' interests; research universities in particular are not demand-driven in the sense that they respond to demand from society. As a result, little attention is paid to soft skills, leadership or IT skills, for example. Nevertheless, these are precisely the skills that could characterize the curriculum of tomorrow, given the completely different role that this knowledge will play in the future. Today, in many respects, there is still an emphasis on the acquisition of knowledge in academic education. But in future, knowledge will be available everywhere in advanced IT systems and the role of the university graduate will shift from gathering and generating knowledge to using it. Both in research and in industry or societal organizations, this will usually take place in wider interdisciplinary contexts, where new scholarship will emerge as a result of the linking of totally different disciplines. These convergences will become a leading form of scholarship,[1] and will therefore also play a defining role in teaching.

In general, we can already see initiatives that incorporate the trend described above. The idea of the 'T-shaped professional' is by no means new, but it will undoubtedly become more important in future. In this context, 'T-shaped' refers to how the vertical column of the 'T' represents in-depth

1   National Research Council, 2015: *Facilitating Interdisciplinary Research*, The National Academies Press.

disciplinary training, whereas the horizontal bar indicates that this disciplinary knowledge is increasingly used in interdisciplinary contexts. Disciplinary training will remain important, however, because this alone will allow for the development of core competencies such as asking the right questions, designing appropriate research and using the right methods. Whilst higher professional education will have a strong focus on specific labour market issues and teaching universities will focus more specifically on the exclusive transfer of knowledge, research universities will have to pay serious attention to the ongoing interconnection of research and teaching, based on disciplinary training. But as research will increasingly become a matter of cooperation between different disciplines, teaching will have to provide thorough training in the 'soft skills' that facilitate this interdisciplinary collaboration.

In the period since the Second World War, university programmes have become more and more specialized, and less attention is paid to the more general formation of students or *Bildung*. The current debate about the university of the future mainly focuses on this broad academic training that students should receive, but as we design the curriculum of the future, it is at least as urgent to reflect on other qualities. The old notion of the university as the place where members of the elite were trained only remains to a limited extent; it can still be found today, for example, in selective and exclusive universities such as American Ivy League institutions. Students at such universities are constantly reminded of their potential future leadership role, although they receive little training for this. In many Western Europe universities, ideas of elites and leadership disappeared long ago as institutions became mass institutions, and this is actually a pity. Many of the problems that we face today and that we will face tomorrow threaten to become mired in the simple-mindedness of Facebook, Twitter and modern communications. Leadership will be particularly important here, certainly in the extremely complex society of the future, when it will probably entail solving major problems. This would allow the university to underline the social significance of its role, but it should then pay specific attention to the development of leadership training – much more than is now the case.

There are major regional differences, of course, that will play a decisive role in how the general developments described above unfold. In parts of Europe and in North America, we have already seen the first shift towards more interdisciplinary teaching, including a focus on soft skills, and this will undoubtedly continue further in the coming decades. The situation in Asia is very different. The dominant notion of the ideal curriculum in Asia is roughly as follows: teaching should be discipline-based, above all else, and it should be a largely one-way process. Lecturers provide traditional education, often in large groups, which is mainly based on a combination of a large number of contact hours with hardworking students. This picture is strengthened by the fact that even in systems that are more oriented towards the West, such as in Singapore, there is notably little interaction between students and lecturers. Evaluations show that the lecturers hardly pay attention to the students' comments, and the latter subsequently feel that they have very little influence on the quality of the teaching.

We will probably continue to see significant differences between the student populations across the different continents in the coming years, as these have deep-rooted cultural causes. Asian students are exceptionally disciplined, competitive, deeply wishing to make their mark, and, above all, they accept authority with little public critical reflection. This means that they keep their opinions to themselves and it is difficult to elicit critical comments from them, even in private conversation. But both in China and Hong Kong and also in Singapore, for example, there is a second element that distinguishes Asian students sharply from their Western, and certainly from their European and Dutch, peers: many of them are keen to enter the labour market immediately after gaining a degree, due to the high level of demand. There is a flexible labour market in Asia, where academically trained graduates are prepared to accept jobs that are totally unrelated to the subject they originally studied. These Asian students also have high expectations of the future, characterized by the image of the social climber. Parents and children make huge efforts to ensure that children have a better life than their parents: students therefore want to get working as soon as possible after their Bachelor's degrees, so they can earn a good income.

More so than in Europe, students in the US are often articulate and trained in rhetoric. They are good at debating in public, certainly compared to their Asian peers. In the coming years, Western universities will be able to draw considerable benefit from the fact that their students' articulate nature lends itself particularly well to bringing research into the curriculum at an early stage, and to training students to think creatively and independently. Conversely, in the coming years, one disadvantage could be that as a result of increased prosperity in Europe in particular, student motivation may remain low and dropout rates high, especially in countries with free or low-cost university teaching. In addition, most students have only a vague idea of their future role in the labour market. This will undoubtedly change, certainly if funding proves harder to come by, and particularly if European universities move in the direction of rising tuition fees and more selection.

In any case, there is one quality that makes the Asian curriculum – with the forerunners again being Singapore and Hong Kong – stronger than those in Europe or North America: internationalization. In Hong Kong, the Bachelor's phase was recently lengthened by a year, and there is a striking degree of interest in and attention paid to spending a period abroad, both in Hong Kong and in Singapore. In Hong Kong, this additional fourth year is partly intended for international orientation. Governments also strongly encourage international exchanges, on the basis that it is essential to have an understanding of the world beyond Asia. This is much less the case in Europe and the US. Despite this, the internationalization of teaching will undoubtedly increase in future, due to the importance of remaining connected to the international pool of talent.

In short, where will the contours of the teaching of the future lie? What will the core competencies be in the curriculum of the future? In addition to disciplinary training (for this will always be needed), the accent will shift to the development of strong academic skills. The emphasis will come to lie more on training students how to ask the right questions and how to extract knowledge from the large data systems and expert systems that we will have in 2040. In this context, it is extremely important to develop a good academic core curriculum that serves these objectives. The American system appears to have a head start in this respect, because it already has a broad Bachelor's phase that mainly provides academic education. But there, too, just as elsewhere in the world, a greater emphasis on leadership is needed, on playing a visible role in social debates, rather than disciplinary skills alone. The image of the T-sł professional will need to be reinforced everywhere, anu will also partly shape the curriculum.

The university's educational mission will thus change radically in the coming years: there will be significant differentiation between universities, the top universities will enjoy a larger share of academic education, and there will be greater emphasis on leadership and interdisciplinarity. Putting all of the above together, a picture emerges that is captured well in the old, now unfortunately abandoned, mission statement of the University of Manchester:

> Likewise Manchester's educational mission goes well beyond the development of highly employable professionals, vital though that is, and places equal emphasis on preparing graduates to take personal responsibility, as citizens, for building sustainable civil societies in the 21st century and addressing the great social and environmental issues confronting humankind. Our idea of a university is of a strong, independent knowledge institution seeking not only to understand the human and natural world, but to bring knowledge and wisdom to bear on sustaining and improving the quality of life on earth.

In recent years, the world has changed fundamentally as a result of globalization and developments in IT, leading to the emergence of a modular economy. Parts of the design and manufacturing process take place in completely different corners of the world and are eventually assembled into an end-product for sale. This latter part of the process – the marketing and sale of the product – can also take place in a range of different places, thanks to rapid connections and good communications. We could imagine a similar trend in education, especially in higher education. Modular teaching is provided in accordance with taste and demand, and will increasingly have to meet the needs of the student. These could be needs relating to time, such as the time periods when a student studies, but also changing needs over a lifetime. Thus there will undoubtedly be growing demand for lifelong learning. But there are also aspects that relate to the organization of teaching, rather than just dividing up teaching into modules.

Modularization enables a student to select individually those parts of the curriculum in which he or she is interested, for which there is a need, or that provide a direct solution to a problem that has arisen. We will see an inevitable shift from curriculum-based education to personalized, customized education. According to Dawson, the learning process will move from the formal to the informal domain,[2] and we will increasingly see phenomena such as 'workflow learning';[3] that is, only learning something if there is a need to do so in response to a problem or question. To quote Dawson: 'This kind of learning is about networks, about access, about critical thinking and problem solving.'

If there is indeed a shift from the formal, coherent curriculum to digital, informal and modular teaching, we will also see a shift in certification. For centuries, the university has derived much of its power and prestige from the conferral of qualifications; that is to say, issuing a guarantee that the individual who is graduating is actually able to do what has been promised and what is expected of them. Students pay for the diploma with rising tuition fees, so that they can obtain a good job in exchange. But the situation in future

2 Dawson, R.: *The Future of Universities.* http://rossdawson.com/keynote-speaker/keynote-speaking-topics/keynote-speaking-topics-the-future-of-universities-and-education/#ixzz3Sm37jL1q.

3 Cross, J., in: Dawson, R.: *The Future of Universities.*

may be very different: students may study for as long as they consider necessary, and may tailor their studies to their own taste and choices, for which certification will be required from the university or another institution.[4]

The later phases of the Bachelor's programme will be especially susceptible to modularization and 'unbundling', and a decrease in campus-based teaching in favour of online education. This will undoubtedly lead to further differentiation between teaching universities and research universities. The latter will only be able to distinguish themselves successfully through the intensity of their research-driven training, which can only really be provided in a campus environment. It will be this latter form of teaching (which private and online providers will find much more difficult to offer) that will put the research university on the firmest ground in comparison with teaching universities. In addition, the research university will only be able to survive if it can make good on its promise to provide the best academic education for the best students, thorough training in research, and produce graduates who are among the best in their generation. Another factor playing a decisive role here will be the speed at which the government steps back and tuition fees rise. Certainly if the government continues to withdraw at the same rate as in recent decades, students will quickly conclude that the combination of university teaching plus making an early start to their career in the labour market is much more attractive than four years of increasingly expensive campus tuition.

In a number of cases, it will be possible to establish a fully digital university; this will be easiest in certain niche areas,

4   Barber, M., K. Donnelly & S. Rizvi, 2013: *An Avalanche Is Coming. Higher Education and the Revolution Ahead*, Institute for Public Policy Research.

such as business administration, law and similar disciplines, which are relatively independent of facilities or laboratories. But there is every reason to assume that there will still be a rationale for the existence of the campus. It is of unquestionable value to young people, especially in the first years of university education, to be educated in physical proximity to their peers and receive real-world teaching with a high degree of interaction. If the trend towards the unbundling of education and blended learning increases, however, as is anticipated, the character of the campus university will undoubtedly change. The campus will no longer be full of teaching buildings, as students will take many courses at a distance and in their own time. The campus will mainly become a place where research is conducted, as well as teaching, and where students meet for a whole range of purposes: to discuss their courses, to prepare for research, but also to meet up socially. Rather than formal learning in which the lecturer plays the main role, the university will have to invest in informal learning, whereby students are encouraged to meet one another in order to support the formal study process in every possible way.

The campus of the future will thus be very different from the campus of today: there will be fewer teaching buildings, more interaction, more culture and more conviviality. In this respect, universities are becoming much more than simple providers of teaching and producers of research: they will return to the formational task that used to characterize the university years back. What is more, once they have completed their studies, the university will become a centre of lifelong learning for alumni, where they can do further training, if needed, and can make use of facilities by means of alumni return schemes. In short: the university's influence will extend more deeply into the life of society.

As suggested above, the campus will be on firmest ground in the research universities: this is where we will always find the clearest rationale for a campus based on links between research and teaching, and thereby often the links with campus-based facilities. Nevertheless, we will also see a rise in blended learning, and having actual physical buildings will become less important. The US is a clear frontrunner in this respect, and will remain so: there, digitalization has partly been funded through the savings made on buildings, and this is certainly something that is also happing in Europe. Despite this, digitalization will be so expensive that it will not be possible to cover the costs simply by building less. Increasingly, this will compel universities to work together in consortia that share the cost of digital teaching, whereby the offering for the students could become extremely broad. In future, the selection of or admittance to a consortium will play a determining role in the profile of a university: there will be consortia of top universities, but also of less renowned ones, and this will count when students decide where to go to university.

What will the students of the future want? Like today, of course, they will want, first and foremost, to follow a degree programme that secures them a good job. Second, however, students will increasingly want insight into choices for the future that are based on broad social engagement. We will see a new kind of student, who is more interested in the future and the role that he or she will play in it, and who will also be looking for a profile with greater utility and connections with the job market. In the US, and especially in Europe, this will be shown by a fall in the number of disciplinary Bachelor's programmes, and in Europe there will be a sharp fall in the number of disciplinary Master's programmes; we will increasingly see broad Bachelor's degrees for the many, followed by specialized PhD programmes for a relative few. One should add, though, that scenarios on demand for doctoral students suggest that their numbers should rise in response to demand, and broad universities could develop a specialized position here by developing a particular focus on graduate degree programmes. Regardless of this, more than has been the case until now, the number of PhD students – given the determining role they play in scholarly production – will be of great importance for maintaining the position of research universities.

Conclusion: the transition to 2040

The university has definitively left its ivory tower, where it had remained comfortably hidden until the middle of the previous century. It is no longer possible to return, despite some nostalgic calls for it to do so. Today's university is situated rather reluctantly in society; being rather unsure of its role, it is navigating between the entrepreneurial university and the medieval *academia*. This book opened with the question of whether the university would make it to 2040. It has become clear that it will certainly be unable to do so in its current form. We can expect great changes, not only in the form and content of teaching and research, but also in the physical make-up of the campus university.

The contours of this transformation are becoming clear all over the world, although the university is often passive, in the sense that it often operates, to a striking degree, with reference to a mission that is rooted in the past, and rarely looks ahead to the future. Knowledge for knowledge's sake often forms the dominant tone, whilst little attention is paid to societal needs. This appears to be truer of Europe and Asia than Anglo-Saxon countries, because in the latter, universities are already playing a more prominent role in society. This is linked to the need for private funding: as governments have taken a significant step back in recent years, private financial contributions have become essential. Viewed the other way round, it is precisely this decision on the part of the state to take distance that has created a time-bomb in these countries, because access to higher education is associated with a growing financial burden, with a stark social divide as the result.

Much attention still needs to be paid to the university's new role, and there is much work to be done. It is clear that the university needs to play a larger role in society in order to retain broad social support. This means that the university will need to carry out a whole range of activities in society that clearly demonstrate what it stands for. This could involve setting up community services, for example, but also the way in which the university as a whole distinguishes itself from the surrounding community and relates to a city or region in order to make a real and valuable contribution there. The deeper significance for the university is that it will thereby become part of a broader system in which knowledge circulates and therefore brings higher returns: whilst the university has an impact on the regional or even the national economy, at the same time, it seeks to achieve broader social returns for its own performance. This could even lead to universities forming associations with large organizations such as the United Nations, or parts of them, such as the Food and Agriculture Organization (FAO), or with NGOs, regions and governments, so as to provide large programmes with the essential knowledge they need to solve weighty social problems. Much more than is now the case, this should be seen as just as important as, or even more important than, the economic valorization that the university will also inevitably continue to need in the coming years, in order to compensate for shrinking state funding.

All of this will demand radical reform of the teaching and research programme, which should be tailored much more closely to the conditions of the future: the university should become a sanctuary for experimentation and reflection on all kinds of issues that will affect society and the labour market in the years ahead. Ideally, research programmes should focus on the cutting edge of major societal and fundamental questions. Interdisciplinary research will inevitably play a large role in these programmes; after all, the questions that will be addressed in future will transcend disciplines, and the solutions to major problems will be found, more so than in the past, in interdisciplinary or multidisciplinary knowledge. Universities will need special qualities to structure research around convergences – that is, completely new partnerships between disciplines – especially when it comes to technical and administrative support, but this will potentially bring major innovations and scientific progress.

Teaching is likewise experiencing a gradual shift from disciplinary or multidisciplinary education to the real training of students as 'T-shape professionals'. In every conceivable working environment, it will become essential to collaborate with professionals from various disciplines, whereas at present, teaching almost everywhere is based on the dominant mode of mono-disciplinary education and expertise. Although it will still be necessary to provide students with a thorough disciplinary training, in any case, there is still far too little emphasis on interdisciplinary learning, working and thinking at present – and that is true of virtually every university worldwide.

Finally, there is a last aspect to the role of the socially engaged university of the future, and this has to do with the students. Much more than is presently the case, the university should pay serious attention to preparing students for their future roles, not only as university graduates in all kinds of professions, but also – for a considerable number of graduates – in their roles as leaders in the society of 2040.

In order to achieve all of the changes that are needed, the government and the universities should engage in a deeper dialogue about the future. Universities often keep the government at a distance, but it cannot be denied that the government has a great responsibility for the future, and this means that it simply has a role to play. It is also clear that detailed performance targets, such as those agreed in the Netherlands in 2012, provide a bad framework for dialogue, because they focus almost exclusively on production: numbers of students, degree of excellence, numbers of publications. Also the Teaching Excellence Framework in the UK is hotly debated and could potentially deeply affect the university landscape.[1] We need new paths for dialogue and, above all, new kinds of agreements. The latter should focus less on the details and leave more room for change and development within institutions. Above all, it would be good if ambitions were formulated for the longer term that could be re-assessed on a frequent basis, rather than a process of almost constant policy revision. For teaching, in the light of all these major challenges, it will be essential to have stability and a long-term vision that is not changed time and again by rapidly shifting political majorities.

There is an urgent need for a less corporate approach to managing universities, although efficiency and expediency are essential and are not bad qualities *per se.* But in Europe and the US in particular, this approach has penetrated very deeply. This has often led to the unnecessary erosion of lecturers' and students' freedoms, reinforced by a climate of having to be constantly accountable, including to government. In this context in particular, the image of the entrepreneurial university is a hindrance: economic returns

---

1   See on TEF: www.gov.uk/governments/collecxtions/teaching-excellence-framework. Also *Times Higher Education,* 2016: Mock TEF results revealed: a new hierarchy emerges. June 2016.

are quickly labelled as the only valuable form of benefit, which seriously undermines the major contribution that the university can and should make to society.

In their vision of the future, universities should focus on having a diversity of forms, rather than striving for a uniformity that is grafted onto the Anglo-Saxon model. Governments, including in the Netherlands, should be aware of the fact that stimuli in the system often encourage such uniformity; for example, if the system strongly rewards the production of articles or the winning of prizes in particular. But this also requires the universities themselves to pay less attention to the rankings, and more attention to various social issues. Notwithstanding all of this, it is essential that a limited number of universities in every country strive to achieve the absolute top positions in order to stay connected with the global reservoir of top talent and knowledge, which will again benefit the national system. In the diverse university system of the future, there must be room for each university to develop its own individual profile, leading to the emergence of a multiform and flexible system that is able to adapt to almost every change.

Although wide access to education in Europe is a great good, it will not be possible to solve the problem of what are likely to be increasingly scarce financial resources by allowing funding per student to fall. In the long term, this will undermine the quality of the whole system. It would be better, for example, to make access to the research university selective, while strengthening other, cheaper forms of higher education, such as higher professional education in the Netherlands, and making it more accessible. The government will play a vital guiding role here; as shown by the situation in the US, by stepping back, the government can pose a threat to the whole system. Within this guiding role, the key thing will be to ensure that students end up in the optimal place for them, in line with their talents.

Teaching will always be a core task for the university, but it plays a specific role in the research university, namely in relation to research. The funding of the two should therefore be linked. In almost every country, there is a system of separate funding flows, and so long as special value is attached to research, this will automatically result in the under-appreciation and under-funding of teaching. In the European context in particular, there is a need to bring an end to the enormous divergences in funding for education: the arts, natural sciences, social sciences and medicine all deserve the same norm for financing, and a comparable intensity of teaching. Major differences in funding should result from the use of research resources and facilities, which can be specified in the lump sum.

In order to make higher education more efficient, there is a need within Europe to strive actively to achieve a university Bachelor's programme with a clear social impact; that is to say that immediately upon completing their Bachelor's, students should be ready for the labour market and a career in society, and only those with the greatest aptitude for research continue to a Master's or doctoral programme. If necessary, this could be achieved by transforming the Bachelor's programme into a four-year programme, in contrast to the mostly three-year Bachelor's programmes that are commonly run today.

The government and the universities should promote regional systems where deliberate connections are forged between institutions of higher education and with other educational institutions, in which facilities and resources can be optimally used, students are able to find the optimal place to study, and expert institutions are optimally embedded.

Knowledge institutions should strive to develop their academic programmes through constant interaction with stakeholders. In the Netherlands, the National Research Agenda is an example of a reasonably successful approach to co-programming through interaction with the public at large: based on 11,700 questions an agenda finally was made with 140 scientific challenges. But a good mix of research should also be preserved by giving stakeholders – universities, governments, civil society actors – equal power in setting the agenda. Europe is far ahead of Asia and North America in this regard, something that could ultimately prove to be a key advantage.

The university will make it to 2040 – but reflection, debate and above all hard work will be required in order to give shape to all the necessary changes.

Bibliography

References in endnotes

Adviescommissie Toekomstbestendig Onderwijs, 2010: 'Differentiëren in drievoud'.

Altbach, P.G., 2015: 'Massification and the global knowledge economy: the continuing contradiction'. International Higher education. Special 20th Anniversary Feature: Higher Education's Future. Spring 2015.

Altbach, P.G., de Wit, H., 2016: 'Will Trump make US HE great again? Not likely', Times Higher Education, November 2016.

Amsterdam Call for Action on Open Science, 2016: https://www.eu2016.nl/documenten/rapporten/2016/04/04/amsterdam-call-for-action-on-open-science.

Arnold, E., Giarracca, F., 2012: 'Getting the Balance Right: Basic Research, Missions and Governance for Horizon 2020'. Technopolis group, October 2012.

Barber, M., Donnelly, K., Rizvi, S., 2013: 'An avalanche is coming. Higher education and the revolution ahead'. Institute for Public Policy Research.

Barnett, R., 2011: 'Being a University'. Routledge.

Belluz, J., Plumer, B., Resnick, B, July 2016: 'The 7 biggest problems facing science, according to 270 scientists'. Vox.com.

Besser, L., Cronau, P., Cohen,H., 2015: 'Universities embroiled in foreign student "feeding frenzy" driven by corrupt middlemen', ABC News, 17 April 2015.

Bok, D., 2013: 'Higher education in America'. Princeton University Press.

Boulton, G., Lucas, C., 2008: 'What are universities for', LERU position paper 2008.

Bovens, M., Dekker, P., Tiemeijer, W., 2014: 'Gescheiden werelden? Een verkenning van sociaal-culturele tegenstellingen in Nederland'. Sociaal Cultureel Planbureau en WRR.

Bradley, S., Migali, G., 2016: 'The Effect of a Tuition Fee Reform on the Risk of Drop Out from University in the UK'. Economics Working Paper Series 2015/16, Lancaster University.

Bush, V., 1945: 'Science The Endless Frontier'. A Report to the President by Vannevar Bush, Director of the Office of Scientific Research and Development, July 1945.

Carey, K., 2015: 'Are we about to see the end of universities as we know them?' World Economic Forum, April 29, 2015.

Cohen, F., 2007: 'De herschepping van de wereld'. Bert Bakker.

Collini, S., 2012: 'What Are Universities For?' Penguin Books.

Cross, J., in Dawson: 'The future of universities'.

Crow, Michael M., Dabars, William B., 2015: 'Designing The New American University'. Johns Hopkins University Press.

Dawson, R.: 'The future of universities'. http://rossdawson.com/keynote-speaker/keynote-speaking-topics/keynote-speaking-topics-the-future-of-universities-and-education/#ixzz3Sm37jL1q.

Den Heijer, A., 2011: 'Managing the university'. Eburon Academic Publishers.

Den Heijer, A., Tzovlas, G., 2014: 'The European campus – heritage and challenges'. Delft University.

Dijstelbloem, H., Huisman, F., Miedema, F., Mijnhardt, W., 2013: 'Waarom de wetenschap niet werkt zoals het moet, en wat daaraan te doen is'. Science in Transition, Position paper 2013.

Dynarski, S., 2015: 'For the Poor, the Graduation Gap is Even Wider Than the Enrollment Gap'. June 2, The New York Times.

Eagleton, T., 2015: 'The Slow Death of the University'. The Chronicle of Higher Education, April 6, 2015.

Elkana, Y., Klöpper, H., 2012: 'Die Universität im 21. Jahrhundert. Für eine neue Einheit von Lehre, Forschung und Gesellschaft'. Edition Körber-Stiftung.

Ericson, 2014: 'Q4 report, 2014'.

Ernst & Young, 2012: 'University of the Future – a thousand year old industry on the cusp of profound change'.

Estermann, T., Terhi Nokkala, T., Steinel, M., 2011: 'University Autonomy in Europe II: The Scorecard'. EUA report.

Faust, D., 2015: http://www.harvard.edu/president/speech/2015/2015-commencement-speech.

Flikkema, M. (ed.), 2016: 'Sense of Serving. Reconsidering the Role of Universities Now'. VU University Press.

Frey, C.B., Osborne, M.A., 2013: 'The future of employment. How susceptible are jobs to computerization?', Oxford Martin Publications.

Fukuyama, F., 2017: 'The emergence of a post-fact world'. NewEurope 8 January, 2017.

Geiger, R.I., 2011: 'The Ten Generations of American Higher Education'. In 'Higher Education in the Twenty-First Century: Social, Political and

Economic Challenges'. Eds: P.G. Altbach, P.J. Gumport, R.O. Berdahl, Baltimore, Johns Hopkins University press, 237-68.

Gibbons, M., Limoges, C., Nowotny, H., Schwartzman, S., Scott, P., Trow, M., 1994: 'The new production of knowledge: the dynamics of science and research in contemporary societies'. Sage.

Ginsberg, B., 2014: 'College Presidents – New Captains of the Titanic'. Minding the Campus, July 2014.

Goddard, J., Vallance, P., 2011: 'The Civic University: Re-uniting the University and the City'. In: Higher Education in Cities and Regions: For Stronger, Cleaner and Fairer Regions. OECD, Paris.

Hawking, S., 2016: 'This is the most dangerous time for our planet'. The Guardian, 1 December 2016.

HEFCE, 2015: 'The metric tide: Report of the independent review of the role of metrics in research assessment and management'.

International Higher Education, 2015: 'Special 20th Anniversary Feature: Higher Education's Future. Spring 2015.

Jaschik, S., 2016: 'Trump victory will be a jolt for higher education", Inside Higher Ed, www.insidehighered.com, 9 November 2016.

King, G., Sen, M., 2013: 'The Troubled Future of Colleges and Universities'. Political Science and Politics, 46, 81-113.

Kirby, W.C., 2014: 'The Chinese Century? The Challenges of Higher Education'. DAEDALUS, Vol. 143, No. 2, Spring 2014.

Lacroix, R., Maheu, L., 2015: 'Leading Research Universities in a Competitive World'. McGill Queen's University Press.

LERU Advice Paper 20, 2016: 'Citizen Science at Universities: Trends, Guidelines and Recommendations.

Lutao Ling, Fan Wang, Jian Li, 2016: 'Urban innovation, regional externalities of foreign direct investment and industrial agglomeration: evidence from Chinese cities'. Research Policies, 830-843.

Martin, B.R., Johnston, R., 1999: 'Technology Foresight for Wiring Up the National Innovation System: Experiences in Britain, Australia, and New Zealand'. Technological Forecasting and Social Change 60(1):37-54.

McGlone, J., 2015: 'Quid Durat? What lasts?', Cambridge, Massachusetts, May 28, 2015.

McPherson, M.S., Bacow, L.S. 2015: 'Online Higher education: Beyond the Hype-Cycle'. J. Econ. Perspectives, 29, 135-154.

Ministerie van Financiën, 2014: 'Interdepartementaal Beleidsonderzoek Wetenschappelijk onderzoek'.

Ministerie van Onderwijs, Wetenschappen en Cultuur, 2015: 'Nederland 2035: trends en uitdagingen'.

Newman, J.J., 1852: 'The idea of a university'.

Nomaler, Ö., Frenken, K., 2014: 'On scaling of Scientific Knowledge Production in U.S. Metropolitan Areas. PLoS ONE, 9.

Nowotny, H., 2015: The cunning of uncertainty'. Polity, 198 pp.

Nussbaum, M., 2010: 'Not for Profit: Why Democracy Needs the Humanities'. Princeton University Press.

Nye, J.S., 2015: 'Is the American Century Over?'. Polity, 152 pp.

OECD, 2009: 'How many students drop out of tertiary education?', in Highlights from Education at a Glance 2008, OECD Publishing.

OECD, 2011: 'Education at a glance'.

OECD, 2012: 'Educational Attainments OECD, 1960-2010'.

OECD, 2014: 'Education at a glance'.

OECD, 2015: 'Education at a Glance 2015: OECD Indicators', OECD Publishing, Paris. DOI: http://dx.doi.org/10.1787/eag-2015-en.

Onderwijsinspectie, 2016: 'Rapport huisvesting MBO, HBO, en WO'.

Pansters, W.G., Van Rinsum, H.J., 2015: 'Enacting Identity and Transition: Public Events and Rituals in the University'. Minerva.

ResearchNed, 2015: 'Monitor beleidsmaatregelen 2015. Studiekeuze, studiegedrag, en leengedrag in relatie tot beleidsmaatregelen in het hoger onderwijs 2006-2015'.

Roth, M.S., 2014: 'Beyond the University. Why Liberal Education Matters'. Yale University Press.

Ruegg, W., ed., 1992-2011: 'A History of the University in Europe'. Volume 1-4, Cambridge University Press.

San Francisco Declaration, 2013: http://www.ascb.org/dora/.

Sexton, J., 2005: 'Dogmatism and Complexity: Civil Discourse and the Research University'. Based upon a speech delivered at Katholieke Universiteit Leuven. Unpublished. February 2, 2005.

Sexton, J., 2010: 'Global Network University Reflection'. Unpublished address. December 21, 2010.

Sexton, J., 2014: 'Access that Matters: Quality Education for All'. Unpublished address, November 2, 2014.

Shearmur, R., 2012: 'Are cities the front of innovation? A critical review of the literature on cities and innovation'. Cities, vol. 29.

Smidt, H., Sursock, A., 2011: 'Engaging in Lifelong Learning: Shaping Inclusive and Responsive University Strategies'. EUA (European University Association), publications 2011.

Stiglitz, J.E., 2017: 'The age of Trump''. NewEurope 8 January, 2017.

Stilgoe, J., 2016: 'Nobody knows anything'. In: Issues in Science and Technology, Summer 2016.

Susskind, R. and Susskind, D., 2014: 'The Future of the Professions. How Technology Will Transform the Work of Human Experts'. Oxford University Press.

The Economist, 2015: 'Excellence v equity'. Special Report Universities, March 28, 2015.

The National Academies Press, 2014: 'Convergence. Facilitating Transdisciplinary Integration of Life Sciences, Physical Sciences, Engineering, and Beyond'. National Research Council.

The National Academies Press, 2015: 'Research Universities and the future of America. Ten Breakthrough Actions Vital to Our Nation's Prosperity and Security'.

The National Academies Press, 2015: 'Facilitating Interdisciplinary Research'. National Academy of Sciences.

The NMC Horizon Report, 2016: Higher Education Edition.

Thomas, C., 2015: 'Competente rebellen. Hoe de universiteit in opstand kwam tegen het marktdenken'. Amsterdam University Press, 213 pp.

Times Higher Education, 2014: 'Super Size Me', November 2014.

Times Higher Education, 2015: 'Keeping the peace'. May, 2015.

Times Higher Education, 2015: 'Peering into the past'. June, 2015.

Times Higher Education, 2015: 'The weight of numbers'. July 2015.

Times Higher Education, 2015: 'More university mergers on the way, predicts legal expert'. August 2015.

Times Higher Education, 2015: 'Social sciences and humanities faculties "to close" in Japan after ministerial intervention. Universities to scale back liberal arts and social science courses'. September 2015.

Times Higher Education, 2016: 'The Californian System'. March 2016.

Times Higher Education, 2016: 'Europe's 200 best universities: who is at the top in 2016?', March 2016.

Times Higher Education, 2016: 'The California dream is still golden'. March 2016.

Times Higher Education, 2016: 'With greater participation even "greater" inequality'. June, 2016.

Times Higher Education, 2016: Mock TEF results revealed: a new hierarchy emerges. June 2016.

Times Higher Education, 2016: 'Will "anti-science" Trump harm US research?', November 2016.

UNESCO, 2015: 'Science Report, 2015: Towards 2030'. www.unesco.org.

Van der Wende, Marijk, 2015: 'International Academic Mobility: Towards a Concentration of the Minds in Europe', The European Review, vol. 23, pp. 70–88.

Van Rinsum, H., De Ruijter, A., 2010: 'Van Primus inter pares in de Universitas tot chief executive officer in de McUniversity: de decaan als hybride functionaris'. In L.J. Dorsman, P.J. Knegtmans (eds), Het universitaire bedrijf in Nederland, over professionalisering van onderzoek, onderwijs, bestuur en beheer, pp. 37-53. Hilversum: Verloren publishers.

Vedder, R., 2016: 'Mr. Trump: 12 ways to reform higher education', Forbes, http://www.forbes.com/sites/ccap/2016/12/20/mr-trump-12 -ways-to-reform-higher-education/#9087ba479a00.

VERA, 2015: 'Policy brief: Evolving Dimensions of the European research and Innovation Landscape'.

Verbrugge, A., Van Baardwijk, J., (eds), 2014: 'Waartoe is de universiteit op aarde?' Boom.

Von Humboldt, W., 1810: 'Ueber die innere und äußere Organisation der höheren wissenschaftlichen Anstalten in Berlin'.

VSNU, 2012: 'Prestaties in perspectief. Trendrapportage universiteiten 2000-2020'.

Wernli, D., Darbellay, F., 2016: 'Interdisciplinarity and the 21st century research-intensive university'. LERU position paper 2016.

Wilsdon, J., et al., 2015: 'The Metric Tide: Report of the Independent Review of the Role of Metrics in Research Assessment and Management'. DOI: 10.13140/RG.2.1.4929.1363. HEFCE..

Wooding, S., Van Leeuwen, T.N., Parks, S., Kapur, S., Grant, J., 2015: 'UK Doubles Its "World-Leading" Research in Life Sciences and Medicine in Six Years: Testing the Claim?'. PLoS One. July 2015.

World Economic Forum, 2015: 'Global Strategic Foresight Community – Member's Perspective on Global Shifts.'

WRR (Wetenschappelijke Raad voor het Regeringsbeleid), 2013: 'Naar een lerende economie. Investeren in het verdienvermogen van Nederland'. Amsterdam University Press.

WRR (Wetenschappelijke Raad voor het Regeringsbeleid), 2015: 'De robot de baas. De toekomst van werk in het tweede machine tijdperk'. Amsterdam University Press.

Xu, J., Yeh, Q.A.G.O., 2011: 'Governance and Planning of Mega-City Regions. An international comparative perspective'. Routledge Studies in Human geography.

Literature consulted but not cited in endnotes

Adams, J., 2013: 'The fourth age of research'. Nature, 30 May 2013.

AWTI (Adviesraad voor wetenschap, technologie en innovatie), 2014: 'Balans van de topsectoren 2014'. AWTI report 2014.

AWTI (Adviesraad voor wetenschap, technologie en innovatie), 2014: 'Boven het maaiveld'. AWTI report no. 86.

AWTI (Adviesraad voor wetenschap, technologie en innovatie), 2014: 'Regionale hotspots'. AWTI report 2014.

Bakker, M., 2014: 'Onderwijskwaliteit: alfastudies'. De Volkskrant, Tuesday 24 June 2014.

Bod, R., Verbrugge, A., 2015: 'De instorting van de talen aan de universiteit is te wijten aan schraal middelbaar onderwijs'. NRC, Opinie & Debat, Sunday 8 March 2015.

Bommeljee, B., 2015: 'Ondermaatse studenten tegenover slecht bestuur'. NRC, Opinie & Debat, Sunday 1 March 2015.

Borysiewicz, L., 2012: 'Economic growth will come from Europe's research universities'. LERU 10th Anniversary conference in Barcelona, 10 May 2012.

Borysiewicz, L., 2012: 'The Scale of our Ambition'. The annual address of the Vice-Chancellor, 1 October 2012.

Dussen, R.V. van der, Kos, T., 2013: 'Toekomstscenario's open online onderwijs. Verkenning van de mogelijke impact van Open en Online Onderwijs en de strategische kansen en uitdagingen voor het Nederlands hoger onderwijs'. SURF, June 2013.

Eijsvoogel, J., 2015: 'Loopt de Amerikaanse eeuw echt op z'n eind?' NRC, June 2015.

Elsevier, 2013: 'International Comparative Performance of the UK Research Base – 2013'. A report prepared by Elsevier for the UK's Department of Business, Innovation and Skills (BIS).

ESF (European Science Foundation), 2013: 'Science in Society: caring for our futures in turbulent times'. Science Policy Briefing, June 2013.

Georgetown University, 2015: 'Formation by Design'. Project Progress Report 2014-2015.

Goede, M. de, Hessels, L., 2014: 'Drijfveren van onderzoekers'. Feiten & Cijfers. Rathenau Institute.

Icke, V., 2015: 'Onderwijsvernieuwers sloopten de universiteit'. NRC, March 2015.

Kasteren, J. van, Messer, P, 2014: 'Diplomafabriek of wereldverbeteraar? Op zoek naar de publieke taak van de universiteit'. Flux 2014.

Lambert, C., 2012: 'Twilight of the Lecture'. Harvard Magazine, 2012.

Meza, C.M., Steen, J. van, Jonge, J. de, 2014: 'De Nederlandse universitaire medische centra'. Feiten & Cijfers. Rathenau Institute.

Preston, A., 2015: 'The war against humanities at Britain's universities'. The Guardian, Sunday 29 March 2015.

Rauhvargers, A., 2013: 'Global University rankings and their impact – report II'. EUA (European University Association), EUA report on rankings 2013.

Rolvink Couzy, F., 2014: 'De geldwolven van de wetenschap doen gewoon hun werk'. Financieel Dagblad, Sunday 22 March 2015.

Steen, J. van, 2014: 'Totale Investeringen in Wetenschap en Innovatie 2012 – 2018'. Feiten & Cijfers. Rathenau Institute.

Steen, J. van, 2015: 'Totale Investeringen in Wetenschap en Innovatie 2013 – 2019'. Feiten & Cijfers. Rathenau Institute.

The Economist, 2014: 'The future of universities – the digital degree'.

The National Academies Press, 2015: 'Enhancing the effectiveness of Team Science'. National Academy of Sciences.

The Straits Times, 2015: 'Independent learning "equips youth with life skills"'. 11 May, 2015.

Times Higher Education, 2010: 'It's the breadth that matters'. December 2010.

Times Higher Education, 2012: 'Empire and allies'. October 2012

Times Higher Education, 2012: 'Declaration of independence'. October 2012

Times Higher Education, 2013: 'Still personal, still political'. January 2013

Times Higher Education, 2013: 'A different world'. January 2013

Times Higher Education, 2014: 'Hits and myths: Moocs may be wonderful idea, but they're not viable'. January 2014.

Times Higher Education, 2015: 'Last era's model'. May, 2015.

Times Higher Education, 2016: 'Trump election sparks increased interest in Canadian universities'. November 2016.

Trouw, Letter & Geest, 2015: 'Stille revolutie: online studeren'. Trouw, 30 May 2015.

Van der Wende, Marijk (2015). International Academic Mobility: Towards a Concentration of the Minds in Europe'. European Review, 23, pp. S70-S88.

VSNU, 2013: 'Experts aan de slag met scenario's universiteiten'. Toekomst-strategie Nederlandse Universiteiten. No. 2.

Warner, M., 2015: 'Learning My Lesson'. London Review of Books, 19 March 2015.

Weber, L.E., Duderstadty, J.J., 2014: 'Preparing universities for an Era of Change'. Economica.

World Economic Forum, 2015, 'Global Strategic Foresight Community – Member's Perspective on Global Shifts.

Zakaria, F., 2015: 'Why America's obsession with STEM education is dangerous'. The Washington Post, March 26, 2015.

Zhao, S., 2015: 'Price is worth paying for an elite schooling'. South China Morning Post, Saturday, May 9, 2015.